Knife Skills
for Chefs

Knife Skills
for Chefs

Christopher P. Day

with Brenda R. Carlos

PEARSON

Prentice
Hall

Upper Saddle River, New Jersey 07458

Library of Congress Cataloging-in-Publication Data
Day, Christopher (Christopher P.)
    Knife skills for chefs / by Christopher P. Day, Brenda R. Carlos.
        p. cm.
    Includes bibliographical references and index.
    ISBN 0-13-118018-5
  1. Knives 2. Cutting. 3. Cooks. I. Carlos, Brenda R. II. Title.
    TX657.K54D39 2006
    641.5'89—dc22

                                                                    2006007754

Editor-in-Chief: Vernon R. Anthony
Senior Editor: William Lawrensen
Managing Editor-Editorial: Judy Casillo
Editorial Assistant: Marion Gottlieb
Director of Manufacturing and Production: Bruce Johnson
Managing Editor-Production: Mary Carnis
Production Liaison: Jane Bonnell
Production Editor: Lindsey Hancock, Carlisle Publishing Services
Manufacturing Manager: Ilene Sanford
Manufacturing Buyer: Cathleen Petersen
Executive Marketing Manager: Ryan DeGrote
Senior Marketing Coordinator: Elizabeth Farrell
Marketing Assistant: Les Roberts
Senior Design Coordinator: Miguel Ortiz
Interior Design: Carlisle Publishing Services
Cover Designer: Anthony Gemmellaro, Solid State Graphics
Cover Image: Melanie Acevedo, PictureArts/Corbis
Composition: Carlisle Publishing Services
Manager of Media Production: Amy Peltier
Media Production Project Manager: Lisa Rinaldi
Printer/Binder: R. R. Donnelley & Sons Company
Cover Printer: R. R. Donnelley & Sons Company

Text photo credits appear on page 167, which constitutes a continuation of this copyright page.

Pearson Education LTD.   Pearson Education Australia PTY, Limited
Pearson Education Singapore, Pte. Ltd.   Pearson Education North Asia Ltd.
Pearson Education Canada, Ltd.   Pearson Educación de Mexico, S.A. de C.V.
Pearson Education—Japan   Pearson Education Malaysia, Pte. Ltd.

10 9 8 7 6 5 4 3 2 1
ISBN 0-13-118018-5

This book is dedicated to my wife, Tina, and daughters, Hannah, Gabrielle, and Ella Grace, for their undying support, compassion, and inspiration and to Fritz Sonnenschmidt and David St. John Grubb for giving me the passion for food and culinary arts.

Contents

Chapter 4   Knife Safety   66

Chapter 5   Knife Cuts   84

Foreword

Since April 1929, the American Culinary Federation has been dedicated to supporting professional chefs throughout the United States by focusing on education, apprenticeship, and certification. As in any profession, certain skills and proficiencies must be mastered along the way. Certainly one of the most important competencies that a chef must garner is how to use a knife safely and efficiently. Knowing how to slice, dice, mince, and chop is a major building block in developing a career as a chef.

Knife Skills for Chefs is the most comprehensive book on knife skills ever written. It offers valuable information as to how quality knifes are manufactured and the types of knives available. The book's large photographs, coupled with the clear instructions, can serve the student as he or she becomes familiar with basic knife cuts and how to execute them. As an educator, I cannot emphasize enough the importance of gaining knife skills early in one's culinary experience. As a professional culinarian, I know that the knife skills I gained early on have served me well throughout the years. I believe that this text will provide everything a culinary student or an apprentice needs to develop valuable knife skills.

John Kinsella, CMC, CCE, AAC
ACF National President
President and CEO of Kincom, Inc.
Senior Chef Instructor at Midwest Culinary Institute, Cincinnati

Preface

A Note to the Students

A chef told me that there were two things he wasn't willing to share or lend out—his wife and his set of knives. A knife is certainly the most important tool used in any professional kitchen, and developing knife skills will lay the foundation of a successful career.

While we live in a mass-produced world, high-quality forged knives still go through a long manufacturing process under the qualified hands of professional cutlers. This process is outlined for you. Selecting and using high-quality knives will help a chef throughout his or her career. This book will serve as a learning tool to help you select, care for, and use knives.

A Note to the Instructors

This book contains everything a beginning culinary student needs to know in order to select, maintain, and use knives. We begin with a quick overview of the history of knife making and a look at the manufacturing process used in high-quality forged knives. The students are then introduced to the basic knives used in a professional kitchen and taught how to keep them honed and sharpened. Chapter 4 discusses proper knife handling and safety. The rest of the book gives step-by-step instructions, complete with photographs, for making basic knife cuts and introduces students to a number of basic garnishes.

In each chapter, you will find a list of learning objectives and key terms. The definition for each term is given in the glossary. There are also chapter summaries and review questions, located at the end of each chapter. The answer key is found in Appendix VII.

Acknowledgments

For the Book

There are many individuals who have contributed to my success, both professionally and with this book. First, I would like to thank Vern Anthony and Ryan DeGrote from Prentice Hall for igniting this project and keeping it exciting.

This book would not have been possible without the support of Michael Wallick and William Colwin from Mercer Tool Corporation. I appreciate Michael's years of support, guidance, and friendship. He is a true friend and brother, and I will always be a better person for knowing him. William is my trusted friend and colleague, whom I will always affectionately know as "Billy boy."

I would like to thank our photographers, Jim Smith, who did the photography for the accompanying posters, and Jeff Hinckley, who took the photos for the book. I thank the Art Institute of New York City for the use of many of its facilities and students during our photo shoot. Ken Goodman was responsible for coordinating the use of the facilities. His support and loyalty are much appreciated. I thank Eric Pellizari and the Art Institute's New York Culinary Team for their amazing work on knife cuts for this book.

The German photo shoot would not have been possible without the support of Ruth and Andreas Felix. I appreciate their friendship, integrity, and hospitality.

The American Culinary Federation offered reviews of our manuscript and support along the way. I would especially like to thank Michael Baskette and John Kinsella for their support and guidance.

Finally, I would like to thank Brenda Carlos; without her guidance and hard work, this book wouldn't exist.

Professionally

Professionally there are a few people who have helped me find success in this industry. It is a pleasure to acknowledge them at this time for their friendship and guidance. Robb White, Baker College, has been a good friend and is a gifted chef and educator. I have appreciated Ed Leonard, ACF, who has given his support and guidance. Kim de la Villefromoy, Chef Revival USA, is one of my favorite chefs. Not only did he single-handedly change the face of chef apparel worldwide with his innovation and cool designs, but he continually opens my eyes to new food, wine, and restaurants. I would like to thank Duane MacNeill, Chef Revival Canada, for his never-ending support, his friendship, his tolerance, and his thoughtfulness.

In addition, I would like to acknowledge Christian Jarry, World Cuisine, for his fine products and professionalism. Hans Geiser has had a witty presence in my life and shared with me his love of American steaks. And finally, I would like to thank Cosmo K. Day for never letting me down and always being a friend.

Christopher P. Day

I would like to thank Vern Anthony, our Pearson Prentice Hall editor, who gave me the opportunity to work on this book. It has been a pleasure to collaborate with Chef Christopher Day, whose enthusiasm is catching. I want to thank Michael Baskette from the American Culinary Federation for his support and thorough examination of and assistance with the text. I would also like to acknowledge the Art Institute of New York City for hosting our photo shoot. Their facilities and students were both top-notch and extremely hospitable. I also commend Jeff Hinckley, our photographer, for doing a great job. Also, thanks to Kalyca Zarich for her fine assistance during the photo shoot. Finally, I wish to thank my family, who offered support and patience as I worked on this project.

Brenda R. Carlos

About the Authors

Christopher P. Day, considered one of the country's foremost authorities on knives, is the corporate chef for Mercer Tool Corporation, a knife manufacturing company known widely for supplying the majority of fine culinary schools in North America. A 1988 graduate of the Culinary Institute of America, Christopher received his passion for food and cooking early in life working alongside his mother, Patricia, in the family kitchen. In addition to the years spent cooking in New York and Chicago, he has spent much of his career teaching others how to select and use the right knives for the job at hand, as well as how to maintain them. This book shares his years of expertise. Christopher lives in the Chicago area with his wife, Tina, and three daughters, Hannah, Gabrielle, and Ella Grace.

Brenda R. Carlos is an active author and speaker, along with being a regular contributor to *The National Culinary Review* and *Sizzle*—American Culinary Federation magazines. She is also a Pearson Prentice Hall co-author of textbooks on event management, tourism, and culinary arts. Brenda served for nine years as publisher and managing editor for the Hospitality News Group. She is a graduate of Brigham Young University, Provo, Utah, and a member of the International Foodservice Editorial Council. Her company, BC Editorial Services, provides clients with contract foodservice and business editing and writing. Brenda has presented seminars at foodservice industry trade shows and is a frequent speaker to business and student groups. Brenda lives and works in Omaha, Nebraska, with her husband, Rudy. She is the mother of two grown sons and a new grandmother.

Chapter 1

Knife History and Production

Learning Objectives

After you have finished reading this chapter, you should be able to

- Explain the historical development of knives
- Discuss the history of knife making in the United States
- Identify the difference between forged and stamped blades
- Describe the benefits of using high-carbon stainless steel in knife making
- Discuss the steps involved in creating a forged knife

The knife has been described as the most crucial and visible tool in the kitchen. An extension of the arm or hand, the proper knife can help the chef perform at optimum speed and increase the quality of his or her work. The "right" knife not only feels great in the hand and performs beautifully but can last for decades if taken care of properly.

Just as a craftsperson takes the time to gather and learn about the tools of his or her trade, so should a chef carefully select the knife needed for the specific task to be performed. There are a myriad of knives from which to choose. They vary in size, function, blade type, tang, method of production, and materials and come with varying price tags.

Key Terms

annealing

degrading

forging

grinding

hardening

high-carbon steel

stainless steel

stamping

To fully understand the difference in knives, it is important to learn a little about the origin and production of knives.

Knife History

Knives were some of the earliest tools known to prehistoric humans. The first knives were made of sharp pieces of broken stones or bones (Figure 1-1).

FIGURE 1-1 The American Museum of Natural History houses this collection of prehistoric harpoons and knives.

During the Stone Age, humans manipulated the primitive knife by sharpening it against other stones. Later during that era the double-edged blade evolved (Figures 1-2, 1-3, 1-4, and 1-5).

FIGURE 1-2 This is a collage of ancient hand tools. The blades were made of sharpened stone. By 4000 BC, the Egyptians were using knives made of polished stone, such as flint or obsidian.

FIGURE 1-3 This pictograph, from the ancient *Book of the Dead* by Chensumose, shows an Egyptian pharaoh figure holding a knife as he confronts three demons with knives beneath a trussed donkey.

Early knives have also been found with blades made of bone, ivory, horns, or antlers, as well as animal teeth.

During the Bronze Age, knives were made of copper, but that proved to be too soft. Once metal was used, the blades became stronger, thinner, and much sharper.

By 1000 BC, iron was being used. "It was the discovery of iron which gave the greatest impetus to the progress of knife making by increasing the weight of knives, their strength, and consequently their ability to cut," says Yvan De Riaz in the introduction to his book *The History of Knives*.

One advantage of iron was that it was cheaper than the other metals, so knives were soon available to common people. Steel was discovered, and, by the tenth century AD it became the metal of choice for most knives.

Those who made knives in Europe were known as cutlers; they banded together to form guilds by the fourteenth century. About the same time

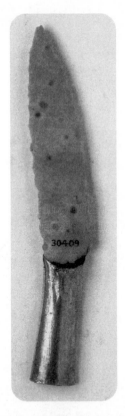

FIGURE 1-4 This ancient Egyptian knife has a flint blade and a handle with carvings showing a battle scene between eastern invaders and the Nile Valley people.

FIGURE 1-5 While the blade of this Egyptian knife is made of stone, the handle is made of gold.

Chaucer, known as the father of English literature, mentioned Sheffield, an English knife manufacturer, by name in one of his writings.

French cutlers had gained world acclaim by the sixteenth century for making some of the finest knives in the world. During this time period, blades were typically made of carbon steel, which could be sharpened nicely, but the blade dulled easily when used. Carbon steel was prone to discoloration and rusted when placed in contact with acidic foods. In addition, the blades were brittle and could snap under pressure.

Blast furnaces had been developed by the nineteenth century, and stainless steel soon followed (Figure 1-6). Stainless steel produced knife blades that were much stronger than before, and they didn't discolor or rust. Getting a sharp edge on a stainless steel blade was a very difficult task, compared with doing so on one made of carbon steel; however, once a sharp blade was established, its sharpness lasted a long time (Figure 1-7).

Today the manufacture of knives has become a high-tech industry, yet much of the process of making top-quality knives is still performed by skilled craftspeople using great precision and care. Most chef-quality blades are made of **high-carbon stainless steel,** which combines carbon steel and stainless steel. The addition of carbon enables the blade to take and keep a sharper edge. They will not discolor or rust.

Sheffield, in England, continues to produce cutlery today. France accounts for 20 percent of the world's total production. Solingen, Germany, a virtual powerhouse in the manufacturing of cutlery, produces as much as Sheffield and all French manufacturers combined. Japan's industry is growing.

FIGURE 1-6 Knife and sheath. This stainless steel knife was made in the early 1900s and are stamped "Wilkinson London & Sheffield."

FIGURE 1-7 A worker makes steel knives by hand in Sheffield, England, during the early 1900s.

Early knife-making history in the United States centers on several individuals who founded companies in the early 1800s. In 1818, Henry Harrington established the first cutlery company in the United States. In 1884, the company introduced the Dexter trade name for its kitchen and table cutlery.

John Russell began the Russell Manufacturing Company in the 1830s and focused on cutlery. Russell enticed English cutlers to come to this country by offering them higher wages than they could earn in England. This brought in a pool of skilled craftsmen. In 1933, the two companies merged, bringing together two respected names in American cutlery.

Knife Construction

Two basic processes are used in the construction of knives: **forging** and **stamping**.

Forging

Forged knives are made out of a single lump of steel, which is heated and put under extreme pressure. The forging process reduces the impurities in the steel, which increases its hardness, density, and flexibility and creates a consistent blade throughout the knife. Forged knives are heavier than stamped knives and provide a better balance in the hand. They are easier to sharpen and, if cared for properly, last for many years.

Stamping

Stamped knives are stamped out of a conical sheet of metal, using molds or die cuts, then ground and honed, producing a light-weight knife. A stamped knife generally doesn't hold a sharp edge as long as a forged knife does. Stamped knives are also considerably less expensive to produce than forged knives, making them affordable for beginning chefs. For most applications, forged knives are generally preferred by the professional chef.

Raw Material

Three basic types of steel are used in the construction of cutlery.

- High-carbon steel provides a tough blade and has the ability to keep a very sharp edge. It is not strain resistant and can rust or discolor. It is no longer readily available.

- Stainless steel is rust resistant but isn't easily sharpened. Once a stainless steel blade looses its edge it can't be repaired.

- High carbon stainless steel resists stains and takes and keeps a sharp edge. Most good quality knives today are made of this alloy, which combines the best of carbon steel. Molybdenum Vanadium steel (a type of high-carbon stainless steel) with a minimum content of .5 percent carbon comes from the famous German steel mill "Krupp." This type of steel produces blades that are corrosion resistant, flexible and sharp.

In addition to steel, titanium knives are very lightweight and durable. They are made using a sintering process and are very expensive. Ceramic blades are also becoming a popular alternative despite their higher costs. Zirconium oxide, the key ingredient used in ceramic blades, is used to create incredibly sharp, rustproof knives. The blade of a ceramic knife should stay sharp for many years, if handled properly. Because the blades are brittler, ceramic knives are better for slicing instead of chopping. There are several disadvantages to using a ceramic knife. When the blade needs sharpening, it must be done by a professional using a special diamond wheel. Due to tariffs and material costs, this type of blade costs considerably more than its metal counterparts. Ceramic blades can snap if used improperly.

Forged Knife Production

To fully appreciate a forged knife, it may be helpful to understand the steps involved in the production. A visit to Solingen, Germany, will allow a close-up look at how chef-quality knives are produced by the Felix Company.

Solingen is home to more experienced cutlery craftspeople than found anywhere else in the world. This is due to the region's rich history of knife

FIGURE 1-8 This old Solingen workshop houses a grinding wheel and is still being used today for knife production.

FIGURE 1-9 The water wheel provides power to the grinding mill.

making, dating back more than 700 years (Figures 1-8 and 1-9). In Solingen in the thirteenth century, swords were made and engraved with the saying "Me fecit Solingen," which means the sword was made in Solingen. Today high-quality chef knives continue to come out of the Solingen region.

The following sections describe the steps used in producing a typical forged and tempered chef knife (Figure 1-10).

FIGURE 1-10   Raw steel is stacked and ready for the cutting process.

Cutting

The raw material is cut to specified measurements, depending on the type of knife being produced (Figures 1-11). It is then placed under 800 tons of pressure .

The cutting process produces metal blanks, which are generic cutouts of the desired shape (Figure 1-12). The middle part of the split, which is wider, later forms the bolster. (A bolster, also called a shank, is the point where the blade meets the handle. The bolster adds weight to the knife and provides better balance.)

FIGURE 1-11   Steel bars move along a conveyor belt toward the cutting machine.

FIGURE 1-12   Once steel bars reach the machine, they are cut into metal blanks.

Forging

During the forging process, the knife gets its rough shape. The raw material is heated until it is red hot to a temperature of over 2,100°F (1,150°C) (Figure 1-13). With three or four hits, the weight of the hammer against an anvil forms the first rough shape of the blade, as well as the bolster (Figure 1-14).

FIGURE 1-13 The knife blank is heated until it is red hot.

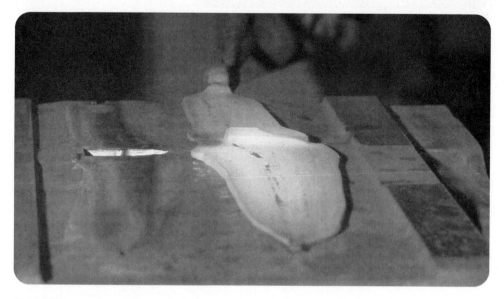

FIGURE 1-14 While the metal is still hot, the blank is hammered into its rough shape.

Annealing

After forging, the knife's blade is very brittle and needs to undergo the **annealing** (heating) process, which lasts for forty-eight hours (Figure 1-15). Annealing consists of heating the material at a low, consistant heat and then cooling it very slowly and uniformly. It takes out the tension and makes the blade more workable, which further enables the forming process. Annealing also refines the grain size, improves the metal's toughness, and evens the thickness of the edge (Figure 1-16).

FIGURE 1-15 Forged knives are prepared to enter the annealing oven.

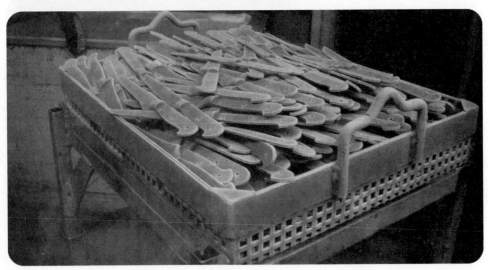

FIGURE 1-16 The knives are cooled after annealing.

Degrading

Degrading is the step used to cut the knife into its correct shape. This is when the blade's shape becomes fine-tuned (Figure 1-17).

FIGURE 1-17 During the degrading stage, the rough forged steel is given its shape.

Grinding

At this point, the blade undergoes the first **grinding** stage, which takes place on a grinding wheel, by hand. The burrs are taken off, and the rough edges are equalized (Figure 1-18).

FIGURE 1-18 Knives are ground by hand on a large grinding stone.

Hardening

The **hardening** process has a major influence on the final quality of the blade and its sharpness. Hardening takes place in four steps:

1. The blade is heated up to 1,920°F (1,050°C) (Figure 1-19).

FIGURE 1-19 The first step in hardening is heating the blade to extreme temperatures.

2. The blade is quickly immersed in an oil bath to further temper the blades (Figure 1-20).

FIGURE 1-20 Knives are placed in an oil bath.

3. Next the blade goes into the annealing oven and is heated to 390°F (200°C) (Figure 1-21).

FIGURE 1-21   A second trip to the annealing oven further toughens the blade.

4. The final step in the hardening process is for the blades to go into a nitrogen deep freeze at −112°F (−80°C) (Figure 1-22).

FIGURE 1-22   Blades are frozen.

Inspection

The raw blade is now finished and is inspected carefully in regard to its hardness, steel structure, and thickness (Figure 1-23).

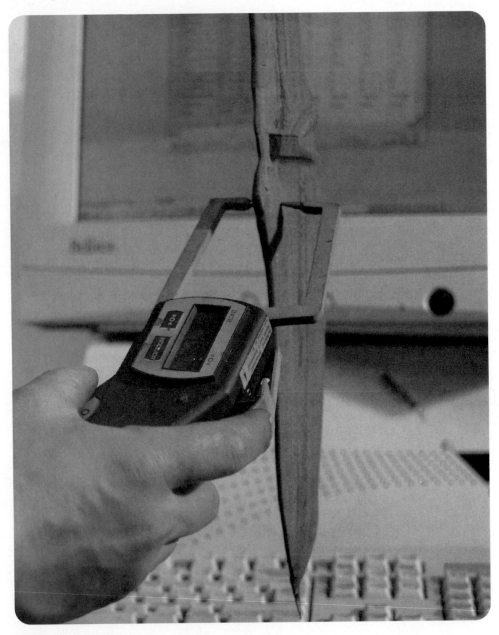

FIGURE 1-23 Using calipers, the worker measures the thickness of the blade during the inspection phase.

Additional Grinding

The additional grinding includes the following operations:

1. Grinding the back (spine)

2. Rough grinding the entire blade

3. Fine grinding, also called glazing—it is during this stage that the blade receives its satin finish; a fine satin finish is one of the major quality marks, because it gives the knife its corrosion resistance (Figure 1-24).

FIGURE 1-24 The glazing procedure is the stage in which the knife receives its satin finish and is done on a grinding wheel with fine grit.

Cleaning

An automatic, ultrasonic cleaning follows (Figure 1-25).

FIGURE 1-25 The knives are dipped into an ultrasonic cleaning bath.

Inspection

The surface of each blade is once again inspected to make sure the blades weren't nicked or otherwise damaged during the additional grinding or ultrasonic cleaning. Prior to adding the handles, the inspector looks at each finished blade to ensure the quality of the final product (Figure 1-26).

FIGURE 1-26 After the cleaning, inspectors select the perfect blades.

Handles

Handles are usually made of wood, plastic, a combination of wood and plastic, or metal. (Check with local health departments to see if wood handles are approved.) The handle encases the tang and is fastened by rivets or covered in plastic or metal.

Most chef knives offer durable plastic handles, which are triple riveted to the tang (which runs from the bolster back into the handle) and sealed with a special method that guarantees that no gaps remain between the handle and the tang (Figure 1-27). Gaps can enable food to become trapped, creating a site for bacterial growth. Uneven rivets can also irritate the chef's hand, causing blisters or sores, and can snag towels and other materials (Figure 1-28).

FIGURE 1-27 The handle is attached.

FIGURE 1-28   The rivets are tightly secured to insure that there are no gaps.

Buffing

The bolster tang and handle are ground (Figure 1-29). Any remaining edges of the bolster are beveled. The edges of the tang are rounded by hand to create a handle that is comfortable to hold and provides good balance. The handle is smoothed, polished, and buffed.

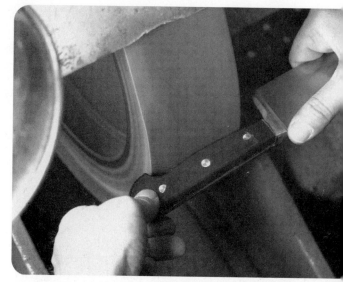

FIGURE 1-29 The sharp edges are removed.

Blade Sharpening

At this point in the manufacturing process, the blade receives its cutting edge by sharpening it against a special stone (Figure 1-30). In this operation, any remaining burrs are removed to make sure that the knife cuts smoothly. A perfect cutting edge will ensure good performance.

FIGURE 1-30 The blade receives its final sharpening on a fine sharpening stone.

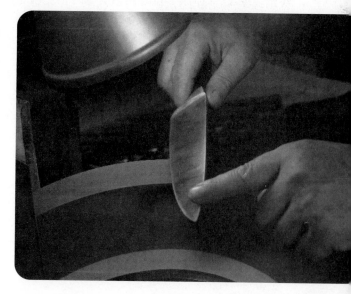

Logo Placement

Blades that make it through the rigorous selection process are stamped with the brand name (Figure 1-31).

FIGURE 1-31 The finished blade is stamped with the appropriate company's logo.

Final Cleaning and Inspection

A final cleaning by hand and a last inspection follow to make sure that only perfect knives leave the factory (Figure 1-32).

FIGURE 1-32 During the final inspection, the blades are tested for sharpness.

Summary

Knives were some of the first tools used by humans. Originally they were made of sharp pieces of stones and bones. As humans made discoveries in metals, knives were improved. Today most high-quality knives are made of high-carbon stainless steel, using the forged method.

Forged knives are made from a single piece of steel, which is heated and compressed under extreme pressure. The steel runs from the tip of the blade to the tang through the handle of the knife. Most professional chefs prefer forged knives over stamped knives. A professional chef cannot afford to be without a high-quality knife. Superior materials and careful construction are the qualities that go into making a knife that will last for years. While the initial investment in top-quality forged knives may seem daunting to a young culinarian, he or she will appreciate it for years to come.

Chapter Review Questions

Short Answer

1. Describe the benefits of using high-carbon stainless steel in the construction of knives.

2. What two companies merged to create the largest manufacturer of professional cutlery in the United States?

3. Why are forged knives preferred over stamped knives?

4. Why is it important that no gaps remain between the handle and the tang?

Multiple Choice

5. It was the discovery of _____ that gave the greatest impetus to the progress of knife making.

   a. fire

   b. iron

   c. steel

   d. forging

6. By the _____ century, steel had become the metal of choice for knives.

   a. tenth

   b. fourteenth

   c. third

   d. sixteenth

7. In the fourteenth century, those who made knives were known as _____ .

   a. cutlers

   b. craftspeople

   c. guilders

   d. forgers

8. Stainless steel was first developed in the _____ century.

   a. fourteenth

   b. nineteenth

   c. tenth

   d. eighteenth

9. Solingen is a leading knife manufacturing region located in _____ .

   a. France

   b. Wales

   c. Germany

   d. England

10. The major disadvantage of the stainless steel blade, developed in the nineteenth century, was that it _____ .

   a. rusted

   b. was hard to sharpen

   c. was very expensive

   d. was brittle

11. Molybdenum Vanadium is a type of _____ .

    a. high-carbon stainless steel

    b. stainless steel

    c. high-carbon steel

    d. ceramic

12. The bolster is the _____ .

    a. metal that continues from the blade through the handle

    b. point where the blade meets the handle

    c. tip of the blade

    d. base of the handle

13. Which step in the manufacturing process heats the blade and slowly cools it, making the blade less brittle and more workable?

    a. forging

    b. degrading

    c. annealing

    d. hardening

14. Which step in the manufacturing process freezes the blade to $-112°F$ $(-80°C)$?

    a. annealing

    b. hardening

    c. degrading

    d. forging

Chapter 2

Which Knife Is Right?

Learning Objectives

After you have finished reading this chapter, you should be able to

- Identify the parts of a knife
- Explain the advantages of various types of blades
- Describe how a knife should handle
- Identify common types of knives and explain their usage

Whether you're slicing, carving, or garnishing, your ability to handle a knife correctly will not only quicken prep time and improve even cooking throughout a dish but will also greatly enhance plate presentation. Knives are made for specific cutting tasks. Using the wrong knife for the job will produce unsatisfactory results and could damage the knife or endanger the user. Using an 8-inch serrated slicer, for instance, to mince a clove of garlic or a paring knife to slice a loaf of bread will never work. It's easy to see how important it is to select the right knife for the job.

Key Terms

bolster	*POM*
butt	*rivets*
cutting edge	*scimitar*
granton	*spine*
heel	*tang*
mandolin	*tip*
mezzaluna	*tourne*
point	

Always determine what you are cutting before selecting which knife to use. The keys to advancing your skills in the kitchen are to select the correct knife for the job and to learn how to use and maintain it properly.

Knife Parts

First it is critical to be able to recognize the components of a high-quality knife and to see how all the parts work together to aid in the process of cutting. Let's start by looking at the anatomy of the knife (Figure 2-1).

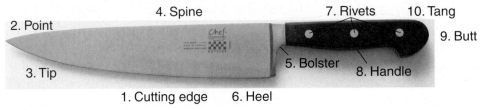

FIGURE 2-1 The anatomy of a knife.

1. The **cutting edge** is located along the bottom of the blade, between the tip and the heel. A chef uses the cutting edge to cut most products. The middle of the blade is used for slicing. The cutting edge can be flat ground and tapered, serrated or granton.

2. At the very end of the blade is the **point** of the knife. It is used to pierce foods, make incisions, and cut small, fragile items.

3. The **tip** of the knife is the first few inches of the blade; it is used to cut small or delicate food items, such as cloves of garlic, onion, and mushrooms, and for cutting thinly sliced soft vegetables.

4. The top of the blade is called the **spine,** or back, of the knife. Chefs often grip the spine with the forefinger and thumb for chopping or cutting.

5. The **bolster,** or shank, is where the blade meets the handle. It is a thick strip of steel and is present on forged knives. The bolster, along with the tang, is what gives the knife a good balance. The bolster also provides a safety feature, protecting the hand if the knife slips.

6. Below the bolster is the **heel,** which is the last few inches of the knife's blade. The heel is used to cut through large, tough, or hard foods when force is needed.

7. The **rivets** hold the handle to the tang (Figure 2-2). Rivets should be flush with the handle to prevent injury to the hand and snags on cloth. When rivets are tight, they prevent the establishment of a breeding ground for microorganisms, which can occur when there is space between the rivets and the handle.

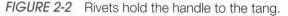

FIGURE 2-2   Rivets hold the handle to the tang.

8. The handle is the final piece of the knife. A variety of materials and shapes are used as handles. Since many hours will be spent holding the knife, it's imperative that the shape of the handle feels comfortable in the chef's hand.

9. The **butt** is the end of the handle.

10. The **tang** is the metal that continues from the blade through the handle (Figure 2-3). Not all knives have a full tang, some don't have a tang at all, and others have a partial tang. The best knives have a full tang, which provides stability and weight as well as durability. Except for knives with sealed handles, the tang is visible in the center of the handle and is securely fastened with the rivets.

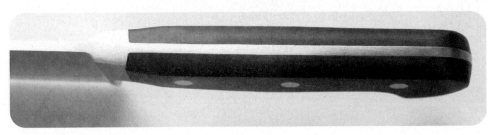

FIGURE 2-3   The tang in the metal that runs from the blade through the handle.

Types of Blades

There are a variety of types of knife blades. Each one has its own advantages, depending on the cutting job at hand.

Tapered Edge

The first, and most common, blade is a taper ground edge which creates a V point. This type of blade is often found in all-purpose knives (Figure 2-4). There are varying stages of taper. Because of the shape of this knife, a chef can cut and chop using a rocking motion. As the blade rocks, the knife remains stable and the work is done quickly and efficiently.

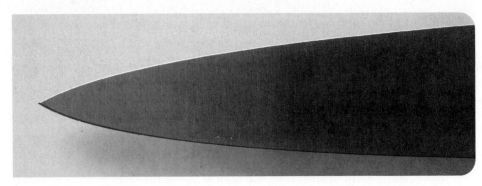

FIGURE 2-4   Tapered ground edge.

Serrated Edge

A serrated edge resembles a tiny saw (Figure 2-5). The teeth grip the food and can easily slice through firm food products, such as a loaf of French bread or a tomato. Serrated edges can also easily cut through melon rind.

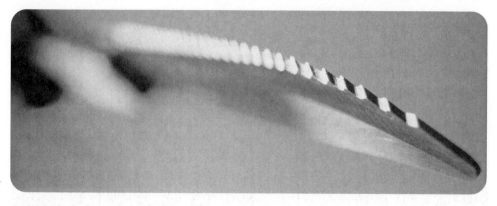

FIGURE 2-5 Serrated blade.

Another type of serrated edge has small scallops (Figure 2-6). It works best with foods that are firm on the outside but soft on the inside, such as many types of artisan breads. This type of knife stays sharper longer than most other blades, because the cutting edges are protected by the points of the blade.

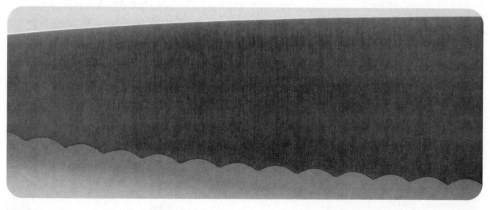

FIGURE 2-6 Scalloped edge.

Granton, or Undulated, Edge

The blade of a **granton** knife has oval indentations, which have been ground into alternating sides of the blade (Figure 2-7). The design of the granton creates air pockets on the blade, which keep food from sticking to the knife. It is an extremely sharp knife. A granton knife performs well with moist meats, such as ham, beef, or fish.

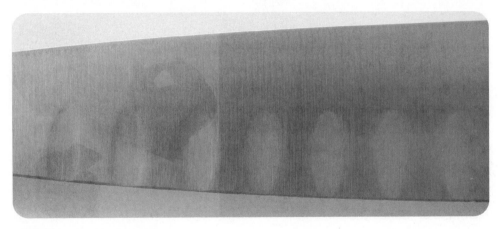

FIGURE 2-7   Granton edge.

Knife Handles

When choosing a knife handle, try holding the knife. Knife handles are made from a variety of woods and plastics. The most common materials used in the construction of knife handles are natural woods and wood composites, as well as plastic (polypropylene) and **POM** (polyoxmethelene).

Wooden knife handles are beautiful and strong, and they provide a good "feel" (Figure 2-8). Wooden handles should be wiped with mineral oil from time to time. Always check with local health authorities to see if wood-handled knives are acceptable in specific jurisdictions. Wood, being more porous than plastic, sometimes harbors bacterial growth. Many of the wood composites combine the benefits of both wood and plastic handles.

FIGURE 2-8   Wood handle.

Plastic handles are the least expensive option and are often used in good-quality stamped knives (Figure 2-9). Plastic handles withstand high temperatures and are durable, they meet sanitation regulations, but they can become slippery to hold. A POM handle provides the same benefits as a plastic one but has a better grip, is more durable, and may last longer.

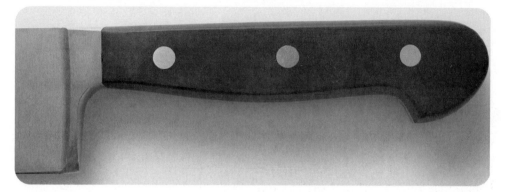

FIGURE 2-9   Plastic (POM) handle.

Knives with ergonomic handles are becoming more popular. These hard plastic handles are molded to fit the contours of the hand, which can help reduce excessive grip force and hand stress (Figure 2-10).

The choice is yours—which type of knife handle would you prefer?

FIGURE 2-10   Ergonomic handle fits the contours of the hand.

Choosing a Knife

How Does the Knife "Handle"?

Choosing a knife is a very personal decision, much like selecting a car or clothes. Since you will use your knives every day, be sure to choose knives that are balanced and comfortable in your hand (Figure 2-11). A chef's knife is an extension of the hand. A good-quality knife will have the weight balanced between the handle and the blade. If the knife is properly balanced, it will feel comfortable in the hand and will be easy to use. The knife should always have an easy grip, which may reduce injury and fatigue.

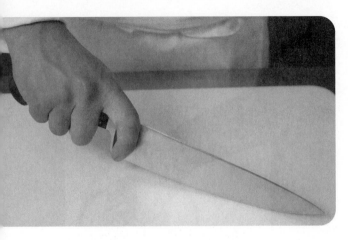

FIGURE 2-11   A knife should feel balanced and comfortable when held.

Quality Features

In many cases, a set of high-quality knives is a life-long investment. A knife should be well constructed, with obvious high-quality features. It should hone and sharpen easily and retain its edge. As mentioned in Chapter One, two basic types of blades are used for culinary knives: forged and stamped. The following sections look at their differences.

Forged Blades

Most forged blades are made from one solid piece of high-carbon stainless steel. The steel is superheated and hammered with a forge into the basic shape of the blade (Figure 2-12).

FIGURE 2-12   Forged knives begin with raw steel that is heated and hammered.

Most forged knife blades have a three-rivet handle and a full tang, running the length of the handle. They are heavier and provide better balance than stamped blades. Forged blades generally have a bolster as well. An exception to this is a forged blade with an ergonomic POM handle. Forged knives are easier to keep sharp than are stamped blades. When deciding which type of knife to use, keep in mind that forged blades are more durable and expensive but, with proper care, will last longer and retain their edge longer than stamped blades (Figure 2-13).

FIGURE 2-13 Forged knives.

Stamped Blades

Stamped blades are die-cut from conical steel, honed, and then polished (Figure 2-14). In most cases, a plastic or rubberized handle is attached. Sometimes a POM handle is used with imitation rivets. Stamped blades don't have a bolster and rarely have a full tang. They tend to be lighter and much less expensive than forged knives, which makes them a popular choice as starter knives for culinary students.

FIGURE 2-14 Stamped knife.

Knife Types

Now that you have a basic understanding about knife production and anatomy, you can look at the many blades that are used by everyday cooks and chefs. You can purchase most knife types with either forged or stamped blades.

Chef's Knife

The chef's knife has been described as the workhorse of the kitchen, because it is used for everyday tasks, such as chopping, mincing, dicing, and slicing (Figure 2-15). This all-purpose knife is also known as a French knife or cook's knife. The most popular length of chef's knives is 8 or 10 inches long. You can purchase a chef's knife that is as long as 14 inches.

FIGURE 2-15   9-inch chef's knife.

A chef's knife is wide at the heel and tapers to a point. The tip is used as a stationary pivot. A chef's knife has a slightly curved edge, which allows for a rocking motion, making it easy to chop, dice, mince, and julienne. The knife's wide blade offers protection for fingers and knuckles.

Paring Knife

The paring knife is much smaller than the chef's knife (the blade measures 3 or 4 inches) and is used for small tasks, such as peeling, trimming and removing the stems of fruits and vegetables, as well as creating garnishes (Figure 2-16). Paring knives are also helpful when paring, mincing, and slicing small items that can be held in the hand, such as a clove of garlic or scallions, fresh herbs and strawberries, grapes, and kiwis. Never try to use a paring knife to cut large foodstuffs.

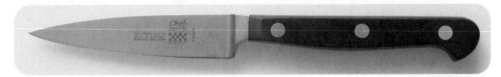

FIGURE 2-16   3.5-inch paring knife.

Boning Knife

When separating flesh from bone, use a boning knife, which is typically 5 to 8 inches long and has a very narrow blade (Figure 2-17). This blade is perfect for deboning poultry, breaking down whole tenderloins, trimming fat, and removing silverskin from various cuts of meat, as well as removing bones from meat and fish. Boning knives have strong blades, which are made to work around and follow the contour of bone and muscle. They come in semiflexible and stiff varieties. A semiflexible boning knife is the better of the two varieties for cutting fish fillets and poultry. The stiff boning knife is preferred for subprimal cuts of meat.

FIGURE 2-17 6-inch boning knife.

Fillet Knife

The fillet knife is used for removing the flesh from whole fish for fillet portions and for producing portioned steaks (Figure 2-18). It is similar in size and shape to a boning knife, but it is far more flexible and therefore ideal for removing skin and bones from fish and poultry. Most fillet knives measure between 5 and 8 inches in length.

FIGURE 2-18 7-inch fillet knife.

Slicer/Carving Knifes

Slicers, sometimes called carving knives, are available with straight, serrated, or granton blades. In general, slicers are long, thin, narrow blades that measure between 10 and 18 inches long. Their strength is in cutting a product that is hard or tough on the outside but soft on the inside, such as French bread and tomatoes, and in slicing meat and poultry. A slicer is the perfect choice for carving turkey, roast, and other large slabs of meat.

Each type of blade offers a benefit to the chef, depending on what is cut. Straight slicers are considered the all-purpose option of the three (Figure 2-19). They are best for cutting tenderloin, whole turkey, or chicken. Serrated slicers, also known as bread knives, are best for slicing breads, cakes, and tomatoes (Figure 2-20). The serrated teeth prevent baked goods from being compressed when cut. Granton slicers have slight indentations on the blade, making them the best choice for slicing whole roasts (Figure 2-21). The more flexible the blade, the easier it is to cut thin slices.

FIGURE 2-19   Straight-edged slicer.

FIGURE 2-20   11-inch serrated slicer.

FIGURE 2-21   12-inch granton slicer.

Scimitar

For chefs who do in-house fabrication, a **scimitar** is an extremely useful tool (Figure 2-22). Most scimitars are 12 to 16 inches long and are made for cutting raw meats and portioning them into a variety of cuts.

FIGURE 2-22   Scimitar.

Tourne Knife

A **tourne** knife has a curved paring blade (Figure 2-23). It is sometimes called a bird's beak knife, due to its curved end, which resembles the tip of a bird's beak. A tourne, or peeling, knife is designed with an arching curve for working on round fruits and vegetables. Tournes are often used to make the classical cut of seven-sided oblong pieces of carrots, potatoes, and turnips used in soups and plated vegetables. Basic garnishing kits usually include a tourne knife.

FIGURE 2-23   2.5-inch tourne knife.

Santoku Knife

Asian-inspired, the santoku knife is an alternative to the traditional chef's knife (Figure 2-24). This is simply a personal choice.

FIGURE 2-24   7-inch Santoku knife.

Cleaver

A cleaver is primarily used for chopping or cutting through bones with its heavy rectangular blade (Figure 2-25). You can also slice, trim, or dice products with a cleaver. The broad, thick blade of the cleaver can also be turned on its side and used to smash ingredients, such as garlic or ginger.

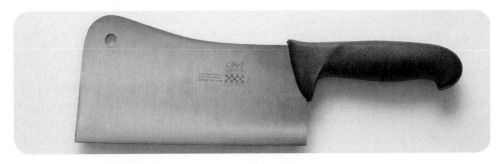

FIGURE 2-25 7-inch cleaver.

Chinese cleavers come from Eastern cultures and can be used as an alternative to the chef's knife (Figure 2-26). You cannot cut through bone with a Chinese cleaver.

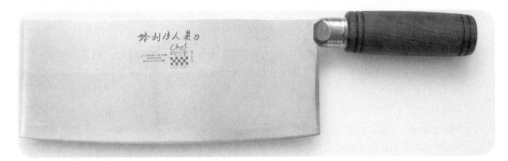

FIGURE 2-26 Chinese cleaver.

Clam and Oyster Knives

These specialty knives have blunt ends and are designed to open clam and oyster shells with their short, rigid blades. Oyster knives have a longer point with a triangular blade (Figure 2-27). Clam knives come with a rounded blade and have one, slightly sharpened side, which can open clam shells better (Figure 2-28).

FIGURE 2-27 Oyster knife.

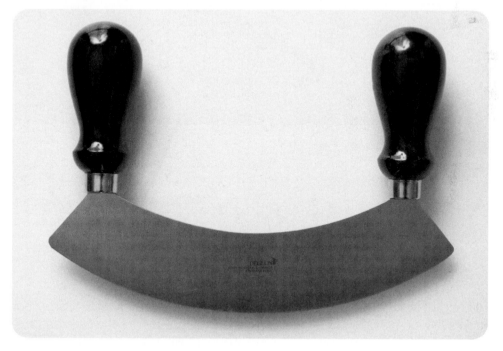

FIGURE 2-28 Clam knife.

Mezzaluna

The **mezzaluna** is a fast and efficient cutting tool (Figure 2-29). It has a curved, sharp blade with handles. Mezzalunas come with either one or two blades. Some people like the faster chopping with two blades, while some think it is too difficult to clean a mezzaluna that has two blades, because the food sticks between the blades. Some models are sold with a shallow, curved bowl fitted to the shape of the mezzaluna. It can be used on a flat cutting surface as well and can easily chop herbs, garlic, onions and other vegetables, nuts, and chocolate as it rocks back and forth. This type of knife has been used for centuries in various cultures. The Italians named it the mezzaluna, but it was also used by the Native American tribes in Alaska and was called the Ulu.

FIGURE 2-29 Mezzaluna.

Mandolin

A **mandolin** (mandoline), or vegetable slicer, ensures that fruits and vegetables are uniformly cut in a variety of shapes and sizes in a short amount of time (Figure 2-30). You can use the mandolin to cut, slice, and julienne and to make gaufrette and batonnet cuts. Mandolins generally have two blades, which can be adjusted for rough-chopping, julienne strips, and waffle-cut and thin or thick slices. High-quality mandolins are generally made of nickel-plated stainless steel with high-carbon steel blades. When purchasing a mandolin, make sure that the blades are sharp and the unit is made of stainless steel.

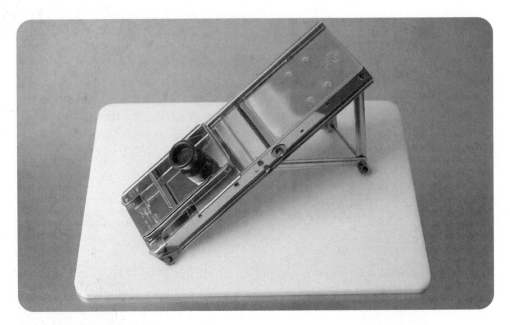

FIGURE 2-30 Mandolin.

Additional Components of Professional Knife Sets

Meat Fork

Although it is not a knife, a meat fork is an additional, indispensable tool in your knife set (Figure 2-31). Meat forks are used to lift cuts of meat when roasting, grilling, sautéing, or anchoring the meat in place with one hand while slicing it with a slicer in the other hand.

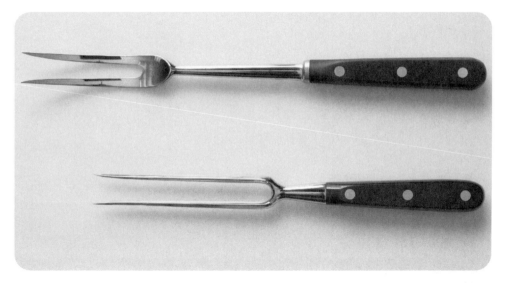

FIGURE 2-31   A variety of meat forks are available.

Kitchen Scissors/Shears

Kitchen scissors can make quick work of a variety of chores (Figure 2-32). Use them for snipping herbs, anchovies, sun-dried tomatoes, and green onions. The best scissors are made from stainless steel, which won't rust and is easy to keep clean. In some models, one blade is serrated, so that the scissors can cut through gristly meat or fish.

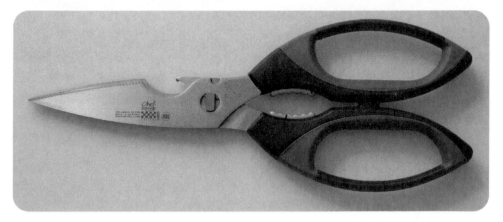

FIGURE 2-32   Kitchen scissors.

Kitchen shears are used for trimming poultry, fish, and many other foods (Figure 2-33). Shears will usually cut through bone, fins, and feathers.

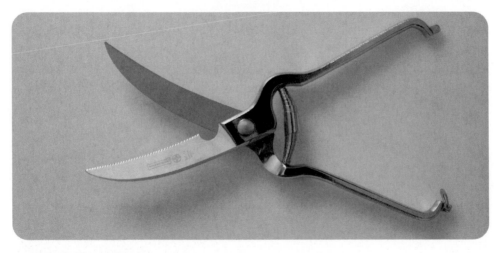

FIGURE 2-33   Kitchen shears.

Honing Steel

Outside of your knives, the most important tool in your kit is the honing steel (Figure 2-34). Honing steel is used constantly to hone or "true" knife blades and is available in versions made of steel, glass, ceramic, and diamond-studded.

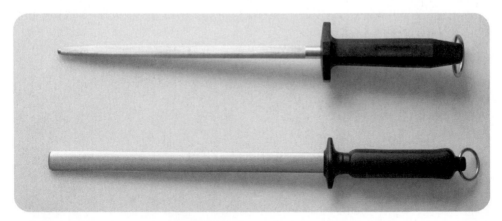

FIGURE 2-34   10-inch steel (top) and a 10-inch diamond steel (bottom).

Sharpeners

A variety of sharpeners and sharpening stones are used to create a new edge on a dull blade. Electric sharpeners are convenient but can wear down a blade if not used correctly (Figure 2-35).

FIGURE 2-35 Electric sharpener.

Manual sharpeners require that the knife blade be drawn across precision roller guides (Figure 2-36). Many brands include diamond abrasive wheels for fast, effective manual sharpening.

FIGURE 2-36 Manual sharpeners.

Oil and water, Japanese sharpening stones, and diamond stones are popular types of sharpening stones. Single, double, and tristones are available providing a variety of sharpening options (Figure 2-37). Once the technique of using a stone is mastered, it enables the chef to control the quality and sharpness of a blade.

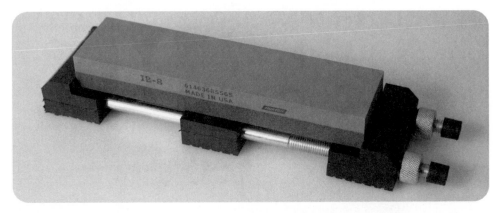

FIGURE 2-37 This double-footed stone offers a fine and a coarse side with rubber feet, which prevent slippage on the workspace.

Summary

Choosing the right blade for the job at hand is imperative and requires some thought and patience. It must be a hands-on decision after testing and feeling a variety of knives as you perform a number of tasks. The right knife will always be the knife that feels the most comfortable in your hand while performing the job.

Chapter Review Questions

Short Answer

1. Why should the rivets be flush with the knife's handle?

2. Explain the difference between a forged and a stamped blade.

3. Describe the three types of slicers.

4. When would a chef use a cleaver?

5. What is the function of a meat fork?

Multiple Choice

6. The _____ is the metal that runs from the blade through the handle.

    a. spine

    b. heel

    c. tang

    d. butt

7. The most common blade is the _____.

    a. tapered edge

    b. chef's knife

    c. undulated edge

    d. paring knife

8. The workhorse of the kitchen is the _____.

    a. paring knife

    b. mandolin

    c. slicer

    d. chef's knife

9. The _____ is perfect for deboning poultry, breaking down whole tenderloins, and removing bones from meat and fish.

    a. fillet knife

    b. boning knife

    c. cleaver

    d. tourne

10. The _____ is sometimes called a bird's beak knife.

    a. scimitar

    b. tourne

    c. Santoku

    d. oyster knife

Chapter 3

Keeping a
Knife Sharp

Learning Objectives

After you have finished reading this chapter, you should be able to

- Describe the difference between honing and sharpening
- Identify the parts of a honing steel
- Show the proper way to use a honing steel
- Demonstrate the steps in sharpening a knife

A sharp knife is a safe knife. With a clean, sharp edge, a knife is more predictable and easier to control than a dull knife. Dull knives require excessive force and can slip off the food and cut the user.

Once you've selected a knife that feels comfortable in your hand, it is important to keep it honed and sharpened for optimal use. Honing steel does not sharpen the blade; it maintains the edge by unfolding it. Honing the blade with a honing steel on a regular basis will enable the knife to cut like new for months at a time. When the blade loses its edge, sharpening is required.

Key Terms

guard	*shaft*
handle	*sharpening*
honing	*sharpening stone*
honing steel	*tip*
ring	

Protect the Blade

The best way to keep a knife sharp is to prevent it from getting blunt. Practice the following procedures to protect your blades.

- Don't cut anything that is harder than the blade of your knife, including bone, unless the knife is a cleaver or was made specifically for cutting bone.

- Never use your knife to cut on a stone surface; instead, use a proper cutting surface.

- Avoid putting knives in drawers where other knives or kitchen implements can come in contact the blade. As a general rule, always put your knife in a blade guard before storing in a drawer.

- Never put good-quality knives in the dishwasher, where the blades can get nicked or affected by caustic cleaning materials.

Many books and guides interchange the terms to "hone" and to "sharpen." This text makes a distinction between the two.

Honing versus Sharpening

Honing is the regular maintenance required to keep knives in tip-top shape. A sharpened blade has microscopic indentations, which resemble small hills and valleys cut into the metal, due to the grinding action of the stone and the pressure applied to the blade during grinding (Figure 3-1). Except in the case of a serrated knife, these indentations are not visible to the naked eye. These hill-like edges curl over or break off as the knife is used for cutting, causing the blade to become dull.

Honing basically maintains a blade between sharpening. The magnetized **honing steel** helps remove broken pieces and realign the remaining ground edges. It will keep a knife sharp for only so long. Eventually, the taper of the knife's blade becomes abrupt and won't hold the hone; this will become apparent when the edge is lost with only the brief use of the knife. There is noth-

FIGURE 3-1 Under a microscope, the knife blade's indentations become visible.

ing wrong with the knife; it's just time to have the knife sharpened. During the **sharpening** process, the blade is reground and its edge is restored.

Knives should be honed with every use. Many consider the honing steel to be the best tool for maintaining a blade's edge (Figure 3-2).

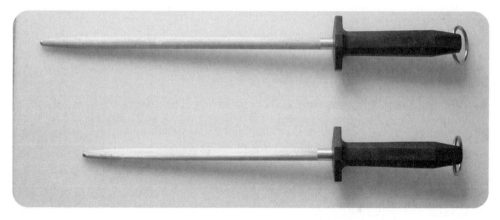

FIGURE 3-2 Honing steels come in a variety of sizes and textures.

The honing steel smoothes and aligns the microscopic indentations on a knife's blade. Most honing steel consist of a coarse steel rod approximately 12 inches long, with a handle at one end. Always use a honing steel that is at least a few inches longer than the blade you are honing. A variety of textures are available for honing steels, including coarse, medium, and fine-grained. Since honing doesn't remove any of the steel from the blade, it can be used without causing too much wear on the blade. (Ceramic- and diamond-coated steels do remove some of the steel from the edge of the blade and should be used with care.)

Types of Honing Steel

A number of honing steels are on the market today. Honing steels are made of steel and ceramic and many are diamond-coated.

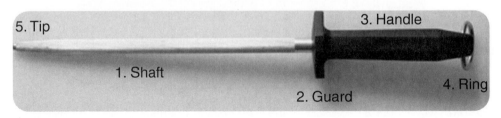

5. Tip

3. Handle

1. Shaft

4. Ring

2. Guard

FIGURE 3-3   The anatomy of honing steel.

Parts of the Honing Steel (Figure 3-3)

1. The knife's edge will be pulled across the **shaft** of the steel during the honing process.

2. At the end of the shaft is a **guard,** which stops the blade from slipping down and injuring the hand when honing.

3. Below the guard is the **handle.**

4. Some models have a **ring,** which allows you to hang up the steel for easy access between uses.

5. At the top end of the shaft is a **tip,** or end piece.

Steps in Honing

By using the honing steel on a regular basis, you will increase the time needed before the blade needs sharpening on a stone. There's some science involved in using the honing steel. Through normal use, the molecules in the blade lose alignment. One advantage of using a honing steel made of steel is that it is magnetized and will help correct this problem.

1. **Use the correct angle.** Most knife manufacturers suggest that the knife blade be drawn across the honing steel at a 22.5° angle (Figures 3-4a, 3-4b, and 3-4c). An easy way to find a 20° to 22.5° angle is to hold the knife blade perpendicular (90° angle) to the shaft of the steel. Then cut that angle in half, so that the knife is being held at a 45° angle. Cut that

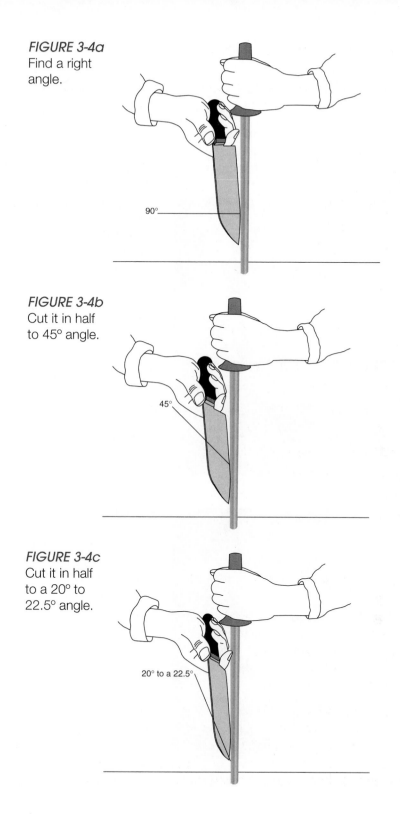

FIGURE 3-4a
Find a right angle.

90°

FIGURE 3-4b
Cut it in half to 45° angle.

45°

FIGURE 3-4c
Cut it in half to a 20° to 22.5° angle.

20° to a 22.5°

angle in half once more, and the blade should be at a 20° to 22.5° angle, or just where it should be held for honing.

2. **Keep the blade at the correct angle.** Continue to hold the blade against the steel at a 20° to 22.5° angle throughout the honing process.

3. **Make five to ten strokes on each side of the blade.** Hold the honing steel shaft in one hand (Figure 3-5). Find a 20° to 22.5° angle and touch the heel of the blade to the top of the shaft. Draw the entire blade of the

FIGURE 3-5 Hold the honing steel in front of the body. Begin by placing the heel of the blade at a 20° to 22.5° angle at the top of the steel.

FIGURE 3-6 The blade is being drawn down the shaft. In this photo, it is halfway through the swipe, and the center of the blade is touching the steel.

FIGURE 3-7 The first swipe is complete as the tip of the blade is drawn above the guard of the steel.

FIGURE 3-8 The process is repeated on the opposite side of the blade.

knife down the shaft in a sweeping motion, so that the tip of the blade ends up on the shaft just above the guard (Figures 3-6 and 3-7). A spokesperson for the knife manufacturing company, Wusthof, describes the motion as "shaving off the surface of the honing steel itself." Use a soft touch; don't grind the blade. Then repeat the process on the other side of the blade (Figure 3-8). Continue to alternate until each side has been stroked between five and ten times. Always work in one direction. Some chefs listen for the light ringing sound that occurs when the blade is held at the proper angle and lightly swiped down the honing steel.

Sharpening

Over a period of time, enough metal will be removed through the honing process and through regular use of the knife that the edge will require **sharpening** by grinding. A number of products can be used to sharpen knives. Some chefs prefer to send their knives out to a professional using a sharpening wheel which can decrease the life span of the blade due to excessive wear and tear on the blade's surface. Other chefs like the convenience of sharpening in-house and have become quite proficient at it.

Stones

The primary tool used for sharpening is the stone. **Sharpening stones** come in a variety of styles and coarseness. Most stones have a different texture available on each side of the stone, from coarse to fine.

- **Double-sided footed stone** is also a common sharpening stone. This sharpener has two sides; one side has medium-fine grit, and the other side is coarse (Figure 3-9). This type of stone sits on an adjustable rubber-footed stand, which allows for sharpening a blade safely without the stone slipping on the work surface. Water or oil is added directly to the stone.

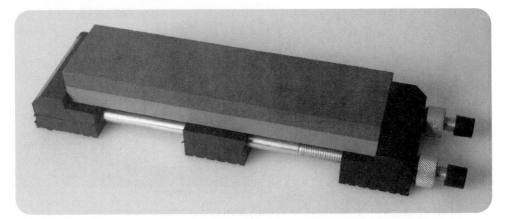

FIGURE 3-9 Double-sided footed stone has two sides with two choices of grit.

- **Tri-stone** is an excellent sharpener and is commonly used by chefs, foodservice professionals, and culinary students. Tri-stones have three sides; each side has a different grit, ranging from fine to coarse (Figure 3-10). The stone sits in a stand filled with a food-grade mineral oil. The oil not only lubricates the stone, which decreases heat and friction, but also pulls metal particles off the stone after sharpening.

FIGURE 3-10 Tri-stone sharpeners have three sides, each with a different grit.

- **Hand sharpeners** are useful when the other stones are not available. Hand sharpeners generally have ceramic or stone sharpening elements which sit at the bottom of a narrow guide, where the knife blade is inserted (Figure 3-11). They are not as precise as tri-stone or double-sided sharpeners but can be a valuable tool when access to the other types of sharpeners is limited.

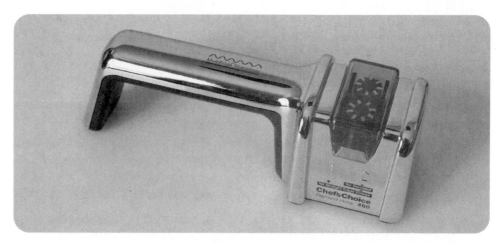

FIGURE 3-11 Hand sharpeners are useful when other sharpeners aren't available.

- **Electric sharpeners** sharpen blades, but they also wear away the surface of a blade and can shorten the life of your knife. The high speed of the abrasive wheels and the heat created when the knife comes in contact with the sharpener are harmful to the blade with long-term use (Figure 3-12). However, many chefs like the convenience, speed, and results that electric sharpeners afford and use them when time is of the essence.

FIGURE 3-12   Electric sharpeners are fast and convenient but must be used with care to not wear down the blade.

Steps in Sharpening a Knife

Follow these steps for a sharp knife:

1. **Secure the sharpening stone.** Place the sharpening stone on a wet kitchen towel or rubber mat, so that it won't slide around the bench or table top.

2. **Inspect the blade.** To determine where to begin in the sharpening process, take a good look at the blade. If it's very dull or damaged, with visible nicks or rough edges, begin with the coarse grit side of the stone and work the blade. If the knife is somewhat sharp and appears in good condition, use only the fine grit side of the sharpener.

3. **Prepare the stone.** Although most high-quality sharpening stones are presoaked with lubricating mineral oil at the factory, it is still recommended to coat the stone with either food-grade mineral oil or

water before each sharpening session. (Water stones should be soaked in water for at least ten minutes prior to use.) To apply oil, simply drizzle a thin layer across the stone (Figure 3-13). Do not use both oil and water at the same time—choose one. Vegetable oil and olive oil are not recommended, as they gum up on the stone and will eventually become rancid.

FIGURE 3-13 Drizzle oil or water in a thin layer across the stone.

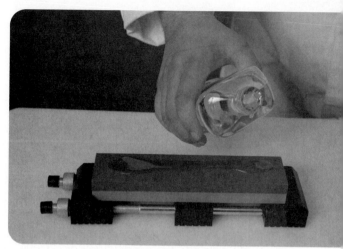

4. **Find and maintain the correct angle.** Much like honing, the blade should be held at a 20° to 22.5° angle against the stone (Figure 3-14). Place the blade of the knife near the heel on the surface of the stone. Holding the knife constantly at the proper angle is the key when using a sharpening tool.

FIGURE 3-14 Begin by placing the heel of the blade on the stone at a 20° to 22.5° angle.

5. **Use even strokes.** Draw the knife toward you from heel to tip, using light, even strokes and maintaining light, even pressure (Figure 3-15).

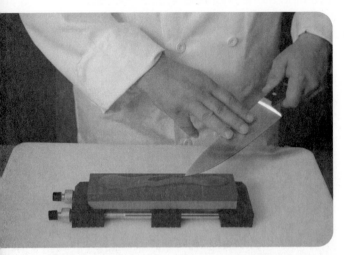

FIGURE 3-15 Use light even strokes.

6. **Repeat on the other side.** Turn the blade over and start with the tip of the blade at a 20° to 22.5° angle (Figure 3-16). Push the blade away from you while maintaining slight pressure. Always go in one direction; never move the blade back and forth along the stone and never sharpen a blade using a circular motion.

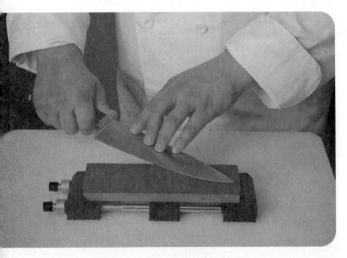

FIGURE 3-16 Turn the blade over and repeat the sharpening process.

7. **Adjust the grit.** As the knife sharpens, move slowly from the coarser grit side to the fine grit side of the sharpening stone.

8. **Continue stroking.** Repeat the process ten to twenty times until the blade is sharp.

9. **Use the honing steel.** The final stage is to use the honing steel to remove any particles left from sharpening before washing, sanitizing, and using (Figure 3-17). Use a dozen light, even strokes, keeping the blade at a constant 20° to 22.5° angle on the steel. Alternate both sides of the knife and steel. Remember that, if you use your honing steel regularly, you'll rarely need to use your sharpening stone.

FIGURE 3-17 Finish sharpening by using the honing steel.

10. **Check for sharpness.** Oversharpening the blade will reduce the life of your knife, as it will prematurely wear down the side of the blade and the bolster. To check if the blade is sharpened to your satisfaction, try cutting or chopping a food product (Figure 3-18). A sharp knife will flow freely through the item.

FIGURE 3-18 The best way to check a knife's sharpness is to use it.

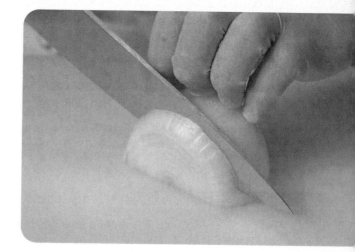

Summary

Using a honing steel realigns the microscopic teeth on the blade of the knife. It should be done on a regular basis. Eventually, the edge will become abrupt and won't hold the hone. At this point, the blade should be sharpened. Always keep the blade at a 20° to 22.5° angle against the steel when honing or against the stone when sharpening.

By following the steps presented in this chapter for honing and sharpening on a regular basis, your blade should have a long, productive life. With a little practice, you will be able keep your knives honed and sharpened, performing at their prime.

Chapter Review Questions

Short Answer

1. List three ways to prevent a knife from getting dull.

2. What is the difference between honing and sharpening?

3. What is the advantage of using a honing steel made of steel?

4. What are the signs that a knife needs sharpening rather than honing?

5. Can a knife be oversharpened? Explain your answer.

6. What is the purpose of using water or oil with a sharpening stone?

7. Describe a method to find the correct angle for the blade on the steel shaft during the honing process.

Multiple Choice

8. How often should a knife be honed?

   a. once a day

   b. whenever it feels dull

   c. once a week

   d. every time it is used

9. Which is NOT a part of the steel?

    a. shaft

    b. guard

    c. tang

    d. handle

10. Which is NOT a reason to use the coarse grit side of a sharpening stone?

    a. the blade is very dull

    b. the blade has visible nicks

    c. the blade appears to be in good condition

    d. the blade has rough edges

11. How many strokes should be given for each side of the blade on a sharpening stone?

    a. ten strokes

    b. fifteen strokes

    c. twenty strokes

    d. until it is sharp

12. What type of oil is best for lubricating a sharpening stone?

    a. vegetable oil

    b. water-based oil

    c. food-grade mineral oil

    d. mineral spirits

Chapter 4

Knife Safety

Learning Objectives

After you have finished reading this chapter, you should be able to

- Discuss why a dull knife is less safe than a sharp knife
- Describe the proper method for checking a blade's sharpness
- Demonstrate the proper method of handing a knife to another person and transporting it correctly
- Identify the steps needed to wash a knife
- Discuss what steps should be taken to treat small knife wounds

A knife is not only one of the most useful tools in the kitchen but also one of the most dangerous. Good maintenance of your knife will protect this investment for many years. Proper use and handling are equally as important to ensure kitchen safety.

antibacterial   *sanitize*

finger cot   *sheath*

pocket roll cases

Knife Selection

One of the easiest ways to avoid knife accidents in the kitchen is to select the right knife for the job (Figure 4-1).

FIGURE 4-1   Using the wrong knife for the job is not only inefficient but dangerous as well. This tourne knife can't carve a smoked turkey properly.

- Use paring knives for paring, a chef's knife for chopping or mincing, a slicing knife for slicing, and so forth.

- Never use a knife to open cans or bottles (Figure 4-2).

- Never use the same knife when switching from meat to vegetables or from raw to cooked foods unless the knife has been thoroughly washed, rinsed, and sanitized between jobs.

Sharpened Knives

- Keep knives sharp (Figure 4-3). A sharp knife will cut quickly and efficiently and with little force. Inadequately sharpened knives are inclined to drag and slip. Learn the proper technique for both honing and sharpening. (See Chapter Three.)

FIGURE 4-3 Sharpening a knife on a wet stone.

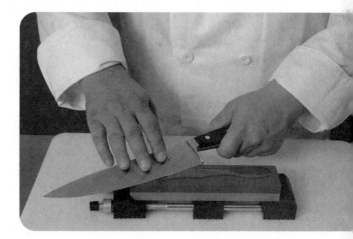

- Don't run your fingers on the blade to check for sharpness. You will know if the knife is sharp by the way it feels as it glides through the food you are cutting.

Usage

Learn the proper way to grip a knife and hold onto the food being cut (Figure 4-4).

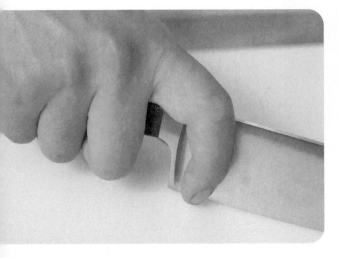

FIGURE 4-4 Use the thumb and index finger on the opposite sides of the blade and hold the knife around the bolster; wrap the remaining fingers around the handle. The knife should be an extension of the hand.

- Always hold the knife by the handle, never by the blade.

- When cutting, know what to do with your other hand. The fingertips should be curled down over the food being cut (Figure 4-5). Maintain a

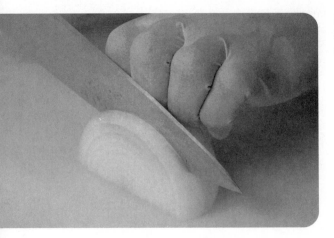

FIGURE 4-5 Always keep fingers and thumbs out of the way of the cutting line.

solid grip on what you're cutting. Keep fingers and thumbs out of the way of the cutting line. Always cut away from your body. Don't cut with the edge pointing toward you or your fingers. If you slip, the blade could easily cut you. Always pay attention to where the edge of your blade is pointing. With a few exceptions, such as making a specific tourne cut or when using a paring knife to peel certain vegetables, never cut any product you are holding in your hand; instead, cut on a cutting board.

- Use proper cutting boards. Wood (if allowed by the local health department) or polyethylene cutting boards are best. Never cut directly on counters, metal, glass, or marble surfaces, which can cause the knife to slip or slide. This practice can also dull or nick the blade and can cause permanent damage to the knife.

- Keep cutting boards firmly in place by planting a damp towel or rubber cutting board liner underneath the board (Figure 4-6). (A towel will also catch any juice that runs off from what you are cutting and will help with cleanup later.)

FIGURE 4-6 Securing the cutting board.

- Always keep the blades facing away from the table or workstation edge (Figure 4-7).

FIGURE 4-7 Keep blades away from the counter edge.

- Between cuts, be conscious of where you place your knife. Avoid setting it where it could easily become covered by a towel or pan (Figure 4-8). Someone might not see the blade and cut him- or herself, or you may forget where you've placed it.

FIGURE 4-8 Never set a knife down where it can be covered with a towel.

- Don't try to cut while being distracted. If necessary, stop, set the knife down, and wait until you can fully concentrate on the cutting job at hand.

- Clean knives immediately after using them. Don't leave them lying around.

Transporting Knives

- Never hand a knife to someone with the point forward. Instead, either place the knife down on a table for the other person to pick up or hand it to the person with the handle first (Figure 4-9).

FIGURE 4-9 Learn the proper way to pass a knife.

- Always walk with the knife close to your side pointed down; that way, if you trip or fall, the knife will fall into the floor (Figure 4-10).

FIGURE 4-10 Walk with knife close to your side with tip of the blade pointing down.

- It is best to **sheath** (a tight fitting cover) the knife or transport it in a carrier. There are many attractive and functional cutlery cases or covers available, which should be used when transporting your knives—such as **pocket roll cases,** which sometimes include shoulder carriers, plastic blade and covers, or magnetic blade covers, that fold over the blade (Figures 4-11, 4-12 and 4-13).

FIGURE 4-11 Knife case with shoulder carrier.

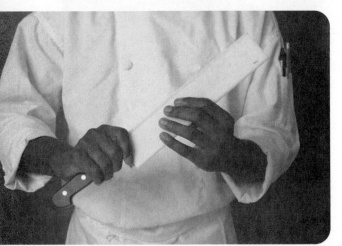

FIGURE 4-12 Blade cover.

FIGURE 4-13 Knife cases keep knives organized and safe. With a compartment for each knife, there's no chance to damage blades by nicking the blades against each other.

- It is a natural reaction to catch a falling object, but always let a falling knife fall. Quickly step away from the falling knife, so that your body is out of the way.

Sanitation

- Sanitation is an important safety issue. Always wash knives by hand. Be sure to wash knives completely with hot, mild, soapy water (Figure 4-14). Harsh detergents can be harmful to both the blades and the handles.

FIGURE 4-14 Washing knife in hot, soapy water.

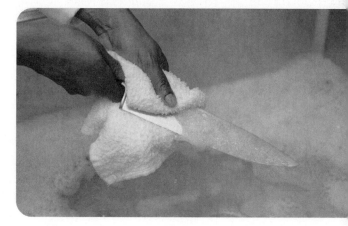

- Rinse with hot water and **sanitize** the knife with approved chemical sanitizers between uses (Figure 4-15). Remember to sanitize the entire knife, including the handle, bolster, and blade.

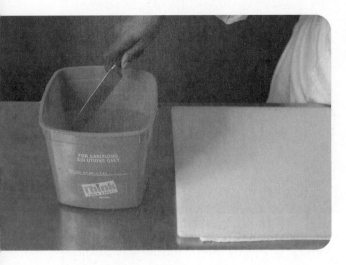

FIGURE 4-15 Sanitize the entire knife including the blade, bolster and handle.

- Don't leave knives to soak in sinks of water where they can't be seen by unsuspecting coworkers. Always wash with soapy water, rinse, sanitize, air dry, and put them away.

- Do not use dishwashers to wash your knives. Dishwashers can abuse knives by banging them around, causing dings and dents. They can also loosen the knife's handle over time. In addition, the chemicals used in dishwashers can cause pitting and dulling of the knife's finish.

- Keep knife storage systems clean. Holders, strips, covers, and rolls should be washed and sanitized periodically.

- Wash, sanitize, and air dry cutting boards after each use. Consider using different cutting boards for each category of tasks, such as one for fish and another for vegetables; this provides a further safeguard against cross-contamination.

Storage

- Don't store sharp knives in a drawer. Uncovered loose knives can bang around in a drawer, which can cause damage to the knife's edge. Loose knives also pose a danger when someone reaches into the drawer.

- There are a number of safe and effective knife storage systems, including free-standing knife racks or blocks that offer convenient access when working (Figures 4-16 and 4-17). Magnetic knife strips are wall-mounted bars designed to hold knives (Figure 4-18). Knife cases are for professionals who want to carry their knives with them. The exterior is padded to prevent any damage to or from the knives. Elastic strips and Velcro-fastened pockets keep each knife firmly in place. Blade covers, or sleeves, are rigid plastic sheaths that slide onto the blade and keep it totally enclosed (Figure 4-19).

FIGURE 4-16 Free-standing system.

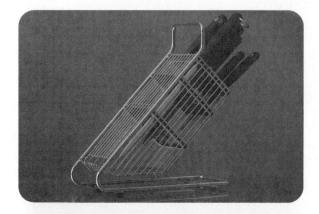

FIGURE 4-17 Another free-standing storage option.

FIGURE 4-18   Magnetic strips.

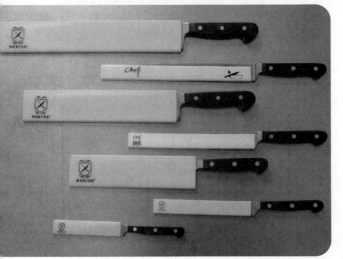

FIGURE 4-19   Always use a blade cover when storing knives in a drawer.

First Aid for Knife Wounds

Even with the proper care and handling of knives, wounds happen from time to time. Remember to keep your fingers away from the blades, use cutting boards, and always keep your knives sharpened. Use these tips for treating a knife wound:

- If possible, rinse the area with mild soap and tap water or pre-packed antiseptic (Figure 4-20). If the wound appears to be deep, don't use soap or antiseptics that could damage underlying tissue.

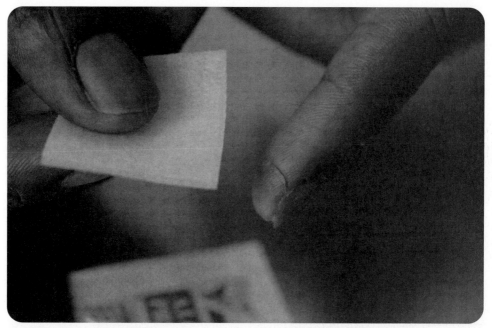

FIGURE 4-20   Use an antiseptic wipe if running water isn't close at hand.

- Apply firm pressure directly over the cut with a sterile bandage or clean cloth (Figure 4-21). If blood soaks through the cloth, place another clean bandage over the top. Don't remove the blood-soaked layer until the bleeding completely stops.

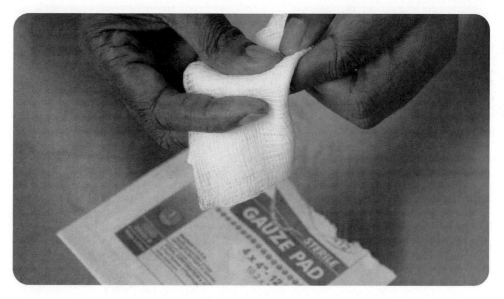

FIGURE 4-21   Use a sterile bandage and apply direct pressure to the cut.

- Once the bleeding has stopped or slowed down significantly, apply an **antibacterial** ointment to coat the wound and prevent infection (Figure 4-22).

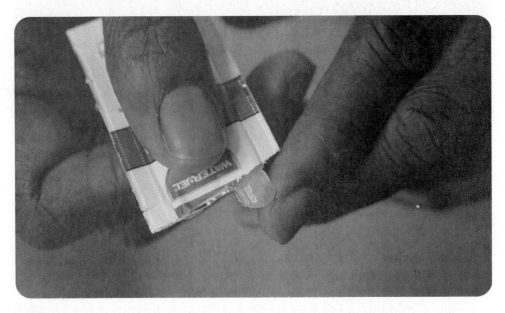

FIGURE 4-22   Apply antibacterial ointment to coat the wound.

- Cover with a bandage (Figure 4-23).

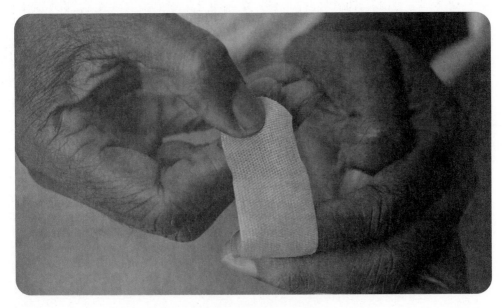

FIGURE 4-23   Bandages should securely cover the cut.

- If the cut is on a finger, use a **finger cot** to keep the bandage from falling off and to offer additional protection to the wound (Figure 4-24).

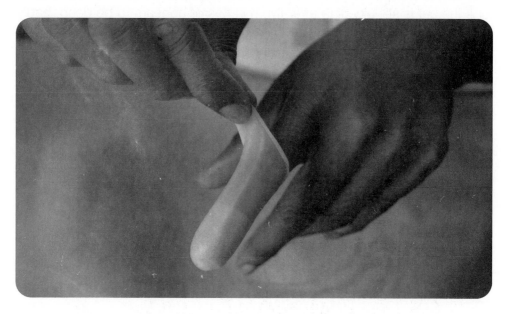

FIGURE 4-24   Use a finger cot to protect the bandage for finger cuts.

When to Seek Professional Medical Help

Seek medical assistance if the wound is still bleeding after five minutes of firm pressure.

You should also seek help if the wound appears to be deep, gaping, or badly torn. A doctor should also be consulted if the wound is dirty or embedded with foreign material (such as dirt or glass), shows any signs of infection, or causes a loss of movement or feeling in the affected area.

Summary

A sharp knife is a safe knife. Keep all knives honed and sharpened. Using the right knife for the job and using it properly will ensure safety. Always be aware of where the edge of the blade is pointing. Always cut away from your body, using proper cutting boards.

Set a knife down on a table or hand it to another person with the handle first. Sheath a knife or transport it in a case. If not, hold the knife close to your side, with the tip of the blade pointed down toward the floor. Never store loose knives in a drawer. Sheath them first or use a safe storage system.

If a cut occurs, rinse it and apply firm pressure. Once the bleeding stops, treat the cut with an antibacterial ointment and cover with a bandage. Before returning to work, cover any finger wounds with a finger cot. Consult a doctor if the cut is still bleeding after five minutes or appears to be deep, badly torn, or embedded with foreign material. A doctor should also be consulted with any sign of infection or loss of movement or feeling in the affected area.

Chapter Review Questions

Short Answer

1. When switching from cutting meat to cutting vegetables, what steps should be taken?

2. Describe a method for keeping a cutting board firmly in place.

3. What is the proper way to hand a knife to another person?

4. Why shouldn't you soak a dirty knife in a sink?

5. When treating a cut, what should be done if the blood soaks through the first cloth or bandage?

6. What are the signs that a doctor should be consulted for a knife wound?

Multiple Choice

7. The best way to check a blade's sharpness is to _____ .

    a. run your finger gently over the blade

    b. try cutting through a piece of paper

    c. see how the knife feels when using it to cut food

    d. try cutting through a piece of string

8. Always cut _____ .

    a. away from your body

    b. with the blade pointing toward the edge of the table

    c. toward your body

    d. with the cutting edge pointing toward your fingers

9. When transporting a knife, walk with the knife _____ .

    a. close to your body, pointed down

    b. with the tip of the blade pointed toward the ceiling

    c. with the blade pointed away from the body and carrying your arm and hand extended

    d. wrapped in a towel

10. Which is the proper sequence for washing a knife?

    a. wash, sanitize, dry

    b. wash, rinse, sanitize

    c. wash, rinse, air dry

    d. wash, rinse, sanitize, air dry, put away

Chapter 5

Knife Cuts

Learning Objectives

After you have finished reading this chapter, you should be able to

- Describe the proper way to hold a knife
- Demonstrate the steps for dicing
- Discuss the differences between chopping and mincing

- Demonstrate the paysanne, rondelle, oblique, tourne, chiffonade, and concasse cuts
- Show how to use a mandolin properly

Ultimately all the care and maintenance of your knife leads to one very important purpose, cutting. Food is generally cut into uniform shapes and sizes to promote even cooking and to improve the appearance of plate presentation. Consistent and precise cuts are the cornerstone of any great chef's skills.

Key Terms

batonnet	*julienne*
brunoise	*mince*
chiffonade	*oblique*
chop	*paysanne*
concassé	*rondelle*
dice	*slice*
gaufrette	*tourne*

Before acclaimed baseball player Rafael Palmeiro approaches the plate, he carefully selects the bat that feels right. Next he takes his stance and does a batter's dance, digging in his back foot until he finds a balanced position—ready to hit the pitch. Before a chef approaches "the plate," he or she selects the right knife for the job and then carefully adjusts the knife to maintain the proper grip. When good balance is achieved between the hold and the knife, the cutting can begin.

Holding the Knife

First the knife should be held in a way that achieves good balance. With good balance, the knife will work for you.

There are a variety of ways to hold a knife; use the grip that feels the most natural or the grip that best suits the job you are performing.

The most common grip when holding the chef's knife is achieved by holding the blade with your thumb and forefinger, parallel to the bolster and placing your last three fingers around the handle (Figure 5-1).

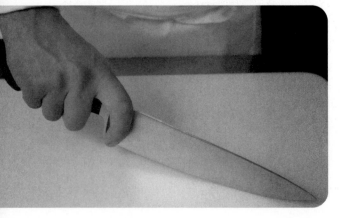

FIGURE 5-1 Gripping a knife.

Some chefs prefer to use just their thumb on the blade above the handle and the other four fingers to grip the handle. The grip will also vary depending on the job at hand. Boning and meat fabrication, for instance, require an overhand grip, with the knife held vertically (Figure 5-2).

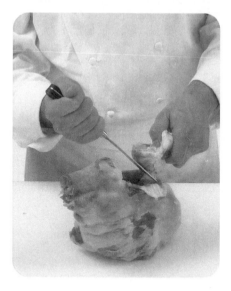

FIGURE 5-2   The chef is cutting a leg of lamb using an overhand grip.

Holding the Food

Use your other hand to hold the food. Curl your fingers back over the top of the product and tuck your thumb in behind your fingers (Figure 5-3).

You can now use your knuckles along the side of the blade to ensure even cuts (Figure 5-4). Bring the knife down with a forward motion to slice through the food product, with the top of the blade on your cutting board.

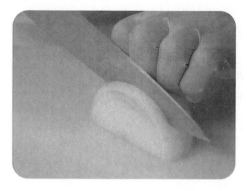

FIGURE 5-3   Guard your fingers and thumb as you hold the food.

FIGURE 5-4   Your knuckles can serve as a guide for even cuts.

Another common grip calls for the handle to be held in one hand so that all four fingers wrap around the handle with the thumb in back. The opposite hand applies slight pressure upon the top of the blade (Figure 5-5).

FIGURE 5-5 Using a rocking motion, the chef chops fresh herbs. Notice how the grip changed for this job. The handle is held in one hand, while the opposite hand applies slight pressure upon the top of the blade.

Note: For best results, always keep the blade in contact with the cutting surface.

Dicing

Dicing is basically cutting a product into cubes with a chef's knife. Diced products are used in soups, sauces, and as side vegetables. Following are the steps needed to dice.

1. **Determine the size** of cube that is needed.

2. **Prepare the vegetable** by washing and peeling (if needed). Next trim it so that the sides are straight and at right angles. It's often helpful to cut vegetables or fruits in half first, so that you are working with a flat surface.

3. **Cut into panels.** Before something can be diced, it needs to be cut into logs or sticks, such as a julienne. Always begin by cutting off one side to make it flat. Next make rectangular slices, or panels, of the product (Figure 5-6).

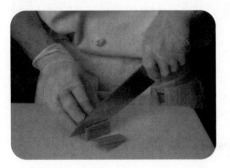

FIGURE 5-6 Cut rectangular panels.

4. **Cut into logs.** Stack a number of the rectangles, or panels, on top of each other and then slice lengthwise, making uniform logs or sticks (Figure 5-7).

FIGURE 5-7   Cut into logs.

5. **Line up the logs or sticks and cut across them again** in the desired size of the cut, creating perfect cubes (Figure 5-8).

FIGURE 5-8   Create perfect cubes.

There are four types of dices, all of which have something in common: They all start out as logs and end up being perfectly square. The difference is simply the size of the cube (Figure 5-9). Until you feel comfortable using these cuts, you can use aids, such as cut rulers and 3-D cut boxes, that ensure proper sizing (Figures 5-10 and 5-11).

FIGURE 5-9   A variety of dice cuts can be made depending on the size needed.

FIGURE 5-10 Cut rulers are a quick and handy tool.

FIGURE 5-11 To test the shape and size of a cut, simply slide it through the coordinating hole on the cut ruler.

Brunoise

The smallest dice is the **brunoise** and fine brunoise dice (Figure 5-12). Fine brunoise dices are 1/16″ × 1/16″ × 1/16″ and a traditional brunoise dice measures 1/8″ × 1/8″ × 1/8″.

FIGURE 5-12 Brunoise.

Small Dice

A small dice measures 1/4″ × 1/4″ × 1/4″ square (Figure 5-13).

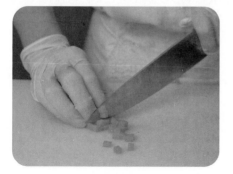

FIGURE 5-13 Small dice.

Medium Dice

Medium dice cuts measure 1/2″ × 1/2″ × 1/2″ (Figure 5-14).

FIGURE 5-14 Medium dice.

Large Dice

Large dice cuts measure 3/4″ × 3/4″ × 3/4″ (Figure 5-15).

FIGURE 5-15 Large dice.

Sticks

A variety of sticks or logs can be made following steps 1, 2, 3, and 4 in the "Dicing" section and omitting step 5. This cut is typically used for salads, entrees, and garnishes.

Julienne

A **julienne** cut is actually the beginning of a brunoise dice and is shaped like fine matchsticks measuring 1/8″ × 1/8″ × 1″ to 2″ (Figure 5-16).

FIGURE 5-16   Julienne cut.

Batonnet

A **batonnet** is the beginning of a small dice and is slightly larger than a julienne (Figure 5-17). It is 1/4″ × 1/4″ × 2″ to 2 1/2″ long.

FIGURE 5-17   Batonnet cut.

Classic French Fry Cut

The classic French fry cut is a variation of the batonnet cut, which varies slightly in size. The blocks can measure from 1/3″ to 1/2″ and are usually 3″ long. For this cut, follow these steps:

1. **Prepare the vegetable** by washing and peeling (if needed). Next trim it so that the sides are straight and at right angles. Remember that cutting the vegetable in half first will create a stable cutting surface.

2. **Cut into blocks.** Always begin by cutting off one side to make it flat. Next make rectangular **slices,** or panels, of the product, creating blocks.

3. **Cut into logs.** Stack a number of the blocks on top of each other and then slice lengthwise, making uniform logs or sticks 3″ long (Figure 5-18).

FIGURE 5-18   Classic French fry cut.

Chopping

Chopping quickly produces odd-shaped cuts. It is the cut to use when size and shape are not important. Start by using a chef's knife and cutting the food product into smaller pieces (Figure 5-19). Begin with the tip of the knife on the cutting board and your opposite hand exerting slight pressure on the spine of the knife; rock the knife into the food product.

FIGURE 5-19   Chopping is a fast cut and is used when size and shape are not important.

Rough-Chopping Cut

Rough-chopping, or coarse-chopping, is often used in making a mirepoix, which is used to season a stock and removed before it is served. The size and shape are not important factors.

1. Clean and peel the vegetables.

2. Grip the knife with one hand and the vegetables to be cut with the other hand (Figure 5-20). There's no need to use your fingers as a guide, since uniformity is not essential.

FIGURE 5-20 Rough cuts are used when size and shape aren't important.

How to Chop Onions

Of all the vegetables a chef will chop, onions are probably the most common. There are a variety of methods to use; select the one that suits your needs.

Method 1

1. When chopping onions, if you want a more uniform chop, start by cutting off the root end (Figure 5-21).

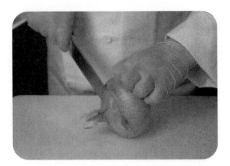

FIGURE 5-21 Cutting off the root end.

2. Slice off the stem end.

3. You can now peel the onion (Figure 5-22).

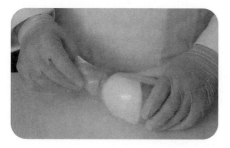

FIGURE 5-22   Peeling the onion.

4. Next cut the onion in half and lay one half on the cutting board (Figure 5-23).

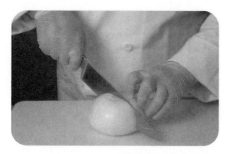

FIGURE 5-23   Cutting the onion in half.

5. Make a series of horizontal cuts, evenly spaced, from one end of the onion to the other (Figure 5-24).

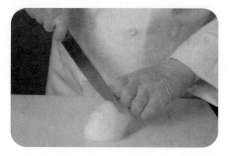

FIGURE 5-24   Making horizontal cuts.

6. Carefully hold the onion together and slice vertical cuts in the opposite direction in the desired width to finish the cut (Figure 5-25).

FIGURE 5-25   Making vertical cuts.

Method 2

1. Cut off the root end and stem.

2. Peel the onion; cut it in half through the stem.

3. Lay each half of the onion down flat on the cutting board. Make multiple vertical cuts running from the stem end but don't cut through the root end (Figure 5-26). Leave about 1/8″ intact.

FIGURE 5-26   Making multiple cuts.

4. Make one or two horizontal cuts through the width of the onion without cutting through the root end (Figure 5-27).

FIGURE 5-27   Making horizontal cuts.

5. Turn the onion 90° and cut through the onion as fine as needed (Figure 5-28).

FIGURE 5-28 Making final cuts.

Concassé

A **concassé** is a fine, rough dice used with tomatoes. Fresh tomatoes are peeled, seeded, and chopped to make a concassé for use in most cooked applications.

1. Wash and dry the tomatoes. Remove the core.

2. Prepare a pot of boiling water and a bowl of ice water (Figure 5-29).

FIGURE 5-29 Preparing boiling water and ice water.

3. Carefully immerse tomatoes into boiling water and blanch for approximately thirty seconds (Figure 5-30). (Very ripe, small tomatoes may take as little as ten seconds.)

FIGURE 5-30 Immersing the tomatoes.

4. Use a slotted spoon or "spider" to remove tomatoes when blanched (Figure 5-31).

FIGURE 5-31 Removing tomatoes with slotted spoon.

5. Immediately immerse the tomatoes in ice cold water to stop the blanching process (Figure 5-32).

FIGURE 5-32 Immersing tomato in ice water.

6. Use a paring knife to peel the tomatoes (Figure 5-33). The skin will easily lift off.

FIGURE 5-33 Peeling tomatoes.

7. Cut the tomatoes in half and remove the seeds (Figure 5-34).

FIGURE 5-34 Removing the seeds.

8. Cut the tomatoes into fourths and chop to finish the concassé (Figure 5-35).

FIGURE 5-35 Chopping the tomato.

Using a Mezzaluna

It's easy to chop with a mezzaluna. Simply rotate the blade back and forth in a rocking motion while chopping the ingredient (Figure 5-36).

FIGURE 5-36 Chopping with a mezzaluna.

Mincing

Mincing is a fine chop cut made by using a chef's knife or mezzaluna. You'll typically use this cut on smaller products, such as garlic, fresh herbs, and ginger.

Mincing Herbs

1. Bunch up the herb.

2. Place the point of the knife on the cutting board and bring it up and down in a rocking motion; repeat the process, moving up the bunch every 1/8″ (Figure 5-37).

FIGURE 5-37 Chopping parsley.

3. Stop before you get down to the stem. Go back and forth from the top of the pile to the bottom of the pile and continue cutting until it is finely chopped (Figure 5-38).

FIGURE 5-38 Continue to chop until the parsley is finely chopped.

Mincing Garlic

1. Wrap a whole clove of garlic in a kitchen towel (Figure 5-39). Using the palm of your hand, apply pressure to release the outer skins.

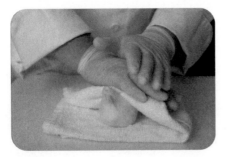

FIGURE 5-39 Wrapping garlic in a towel.

2. Remove the towel and discard the loose skins (Figure 5-40).

FIGURE 5-40   Discarding loose skins.

3. Use the side of a chef's knife to flatten the garlic clove (Figure 5-41).

FIGURE 5-41   Flattening the garlic.

4. Remove the loose skin (Figure 5-42).

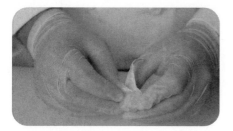

FIGURE 5-42   Removing skins.

5. Place the tip of the knife on the cutting board and one hand on the spine of the knife; rock the knife over the garlic cloves to mince into fine pieces (Figure 5-43).

FIGURE 5-43   Mincing garlic.

Additional Cuts

Paysanne

The **paysanne** is a decorative cut that is 1/2″ square but is cut into 1/8″ slices, so it is thinner than a typical dice cut (Figure 5-44). The final dimensions are 1/2″ × 1/2″ × 1/8″. Paysanne is traditionally a square cut, but it can also be triangular, round, or crescent-shaped, depending on the shape of the vegetable being cut. The key is to keep a consistent thickness for even cooking. A carrot, for instance, will be round unless it has been squared off first.

FIGURE 5-44   Paysanne cut.

Paysannes are like little ceramic tiles and are used in garnishes or when the menu reads "confetti of vegetables." Follow these steps to make a square carrot paysanne cut:

1. Wash and peel the carrot.

2. Cut off the top and bottom; discard or save for stock.

3. Cut into 2″ pieces and square off.

4. Cut into 1/2″ thick batons or logs.

5. Cut across the batons to create a flat dice.

Rondelle

A **rondelle** is a coin-shaped slice of a round vegetable, such as a carrot or cucumber (Figure 5-45). For a more decorative look, cut it on a bias (Figure 5-46).

FIGURE 5-45   A rondelle cut.

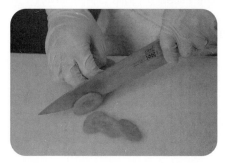

FIGURE 5-46   A rondelle cut on the bias.

1. Wash and dry the vegetable.

2. Peel and trim the ends.

3. Make even, parallel cuts through the vegetable using a chef's knife.

Oblique

An **oblique** cut is used when you need additional flavors and the appearance of larger cut vegetables, as in stir-frying recipes (Figure 5-47). The larger exposed surface area will release flavor more quickly than straight-cut vegetables and still hold their shapes well after cooking.

FIGURE 5-47   Oblique cut.

1. Wash and dry the vegetable.

2. Peel and trim.

3. Using a chef's knife, cut one side of the vegetable at a 45° angle.

4. Turn the vegetable piece around and then cut another 45° angle.

Tourne

The **tourne** is a cut that will take a good deal of practice to master. This football-shaped, blunt-ended cut has seven equal sides (Figure 5-48). A typical tourne cut measures 2″ long and 3/4 ″ in diameter and is used as an accompaniment to a classical entree (Figure 5-49).

FIGURE 5-48 Tourne.

FIGURE 5-49 The tourne cut is generally used on root vegetables, such as potatoes, carrots, turnips, and beets.

1. Wash and dry the vegetable. Peel. (Usable vegetable trim can be incorporated into stock or soup recipes.)

2. Using a chef's knife, cut the vegetable into 2″ sections and square off the ends.

3. Hold the vegetable piece between the thumb and forefinger and, using a tourne or paring knife, cut toward your body.* Cut seven even, curved sides.

   A perfect tourne should balance on end and add a decorative touch to your plate presentation.

---

*Use extra caution, since the blade is moving toward the body.

Chiffonade

The **chiffonade** is a fine-sliced or shredded cut that can be used for salads, sauces, and garnishes.

1. Roll green, leafy vegetables and stack the leaves on top of each other (Figure 5-50).

FIGURE 5-50   Layering the lettuce leaves.

2. Roll up into a cigar shape (Figure 5-51).

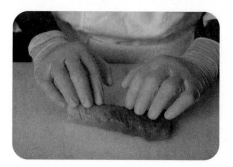

FIGURE 5-51   Rolling the leaves.

3. Using a chef's knife, slice the leaves finely into uniform widths (Figure 5-52).

FIGURE 5-52   Cutting across the roll.

Butterfly Cut

Butterflying (horizontal slicing) splits a piece of meat in half without completely separating it (Figure 5-53). The meat is opened at the slice to look like a butterfly.

FIGURE 5-53   A chef butterflies slices of beef tenderloin.

Butterflying is commonly used for shrimp and chicken breasts, as well as other cuts of meat, and promotes even cooking. The following example shows how to butterfly a beef tenderloin.

1. Trim the meat of fat.

2. Use a fillet or chef's knife to make the first cut. Stop before cutting all the way through the meat by leaving approximately 1/4" uncut.

3. Cut the next slice all the way through the loin.

4. Open the butterflied piece of meat and repeat until the entire loin is cut.

Carving/Slicing

There's nothing more appetizing than watching a chef carve a golden brown turkey or a juicy prime rib in a buffet line. Carving is an art. Use the meat fork to hold the meat in place and a slicer knife to cut the meat into thin, even slabs. **Note:** Cutting parallel to the meat's natural grain sometimes produces stringy results with some cuts of meat. If that is the case, it is better to cut across the grain.

Carving a Turkey

A number of methods can be used to carve a turkey. The following is one to try.

Carving the Breast

1. Let roasted turkey stand for twenty minutes, so that the juices can redistribute themselves.

2. Hold the turkey firmly with a carving fork; pry a leg outward and locate the joint (Figure 5-54).

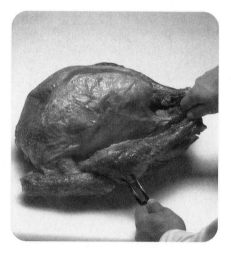

FIGURE 5-54 Prying the leg to locate the joint.

3. Remove the leg and thigh in one piece by cutting through the joint with the tip of a slicer.

4. Remove the wishbone to prevent it from breaking when carving the breast meat.

5. Remove the wing by cutting through the joint.

FIGURE 5-55 Slicing the breast meat.

6. With the leg, thigh, and wing removed, the breast meat can be carved in slices parallel to the rib cage. Slice the breast meat along one side of the breastbone, using long, even strokes of the knife. Remove large pieces, leaving behind as little of the meat as possible (Figure 5-55).

7. Repeat on the other side.

Carving the Dark Meat

1. Remove the leg and thigh (see the preceding Step 3).

2. Place the leg and thigh on a cutting board and cut through the joint to separate the leg from the thigh (Figure 5-56).

FIGURE 5-56 Carving the dark meat.

3. Use the carving fork to hold the thigh firmly on the cutting board, and use a slicer to cut even slices parallel to the bone.

4. Hold the drumstick with one hand, so that the larger end is touching the cutting board. The smaller end will be 4″ or 5″ above the cutting board. Slice the meat off the bone, making sure to remove the hard tendons (Figure 5-57).

FIGURE 5-57   Removing the meat from the leg bone.

Slicing Bread

Slicing is used to cut broad pieces. Slicers have long, slender blades that can make even slices in a single stroke of the knife.

Use a serrated slicer and a steady grip. Slice the bread into even pieces using a gentle, sawing motion (Figure 5-58).

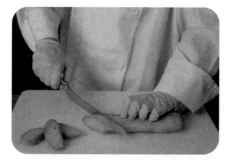

FIGURE 5-58   Slicing bread.

Using a Mandolin

The mandolin is a hand tool that can be used to cut or slice a variety of fruits and vegetables (Figure 5-59). It is a good option when there is a sizable amount of product to be cut and when accuracy is important.

FIGURE 5-59   Using a mandolin.

1. Assemble the mandolin according to the manufacturer's instructions.

2. Determine the size of the cut and select the right blade for the job. Set it to the correct thickness.

3. Place the item you are cutting under the guard against the blade and slide the guard over the blade.

Gaufrette

For the specialty cut known as the **gaufrette,** you'll need to use the mandolin. The result will be a waffle cut (Figure 5-60).

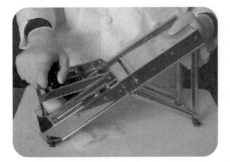

FIGURE 5-60   Gaufrettes are also known as waffle cuts.

1. Assemble the mandolin according to the manufacturer's instructions.

2. Select the ridged blade and set it to the desired thickness.

3. Make the first slice and then turn the product 90° and make a second cut.

4. Turn the product to the original position and repeat with each cut.

Opening Clams

Before attempting to open a clam, it's important to first acquaint yourself with the anatomy of a clam. Clams have a top shell and a bottom shell, which are firmly held together with a tight, muscular hinge.

1. Soak the clams in seawater or salt water overnight to remove sand. (Fresh water will kill the clams.)

2. Scrub the outside of the shell with a stiff brush to remove any sand or dirt.

3. Wear a wire mesh glove on the hand that will hold the clam.

4. Hold the clam firmly in your protected hand and insert the clam knife between the top shell and the bottom shell. Slide the clam knife between the clam and the shell to cut open the clam (Figure 5-61). Work the knife around the opening to cut through the hinged muscle.

FIGURE 5-61 Opening a clam.

5. Open the shell and slide the knife under the clam meat and the shell. Detach the clam meat.

Opening Oysters

1. Clean the outside of the oyster shell with a stiff kitchen brush and wash under running water.
2. Some experts suggest chilling the oysters for a couple of hours prior to opening.
3. Wear a wire mesh glove on the hand that will hold the oyster.
4. Hold the oyster firmly in your protected hand and insert the oyster knife between the top and bottom shells (Figure 5-62).

FIGURE 5-62 Opening an oyster.

5. Twist the knife to pry open the shell.
6. Keep the deeper shell downward as you slide the knife between the oyster meat and the top of the shell. Detach the oyster from the top shell.
7. Slide the knife under the oyster and remove it from the bottom shell.

Summary

After the correct knife is selected, depending on the job at hand, the next step is to learn how to hold a knife correctly. Always use the grip that feels the most natural. Care should also be given to learn the proper technique for holding the food being cut. Always curl your fingers over the top of the product and tuck your thumb in behind your fingers. A variety of standard knife cuts should be mastered. Dicing is basically cutting a product into cubes. Chopping quickly produces odd-shaped cuts. Mincing is a fine chop used on small products, such as garlic, herbs, and ginger. The paysanne, rondelle, oblique, tourney, and chiffonade are additional cuts used for specific purposes.

As a chef, you will discover that your knife will become your most prized possession and the cornerstone of your mastery in the kitchen. As your knife skills develop, knife cuts will become second nature. With practice, you will have the ability to quickly and safely elevate a simple vegetable into a gorgeous work of art.

Chapter Review Questions

Short Answer

Identify the following knife cuts by writing the correct name next to the cut.

1. _____

2. _____

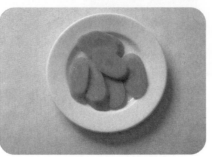

3. _____

4. _____

5. _____

6. _____

7. _____

8. _____

9. _____

10. _____

11. A brunoise dice measures _____ .

    a. 3/4" × 3/4" × 3/4"

    b. 1/2" × 1/2" × 1/2"

    c. 1/8" × 1/8" × 1/8"

    d. 3/4" × 3/4" × 3/4"

12. This decorative cut that is thinner than a typical dice cut and is often used when the menu reads "confetti of vegetables" is _____ .

    a. tourne

    b. oblique

    c. rondelle

    d. paysanne

13. Cut toward the body to create the _____ cut.

    a. tourne

    b. mince

    c. dice

    d. oblique

14. Which is the best knife to use when creating a chiffonade cut?

    a. paring

    b. slicer

    c. tourne

    d. chef's

15. What type of cut is a gaufrette?

    a. dice

    b. waffle

    c. mince

    d. rondelle

Chapter 6

Garnishing Tools and Basic Garnishes

116

Garnishes must be matched like a tie to a suit.

Fernand Point (1897–1955), Ma Gastronomie

Learning Objectives

After you have finished reading this chapter, you should be able to

- Describe the purpose of a garnish
- Identify basic garnishing tools
- Create vegetable garnishes
- Demonstrate how to create fruit garnishes

The dictionary defines the word "garnish" as follows: *to enhance in appearance by adding decorative touches; embellish.* Garnishing is an art, which adds to the color, composition, and overall design of the plate of food. Garnishes are generally edible accents adding visual appeal, which drives sales and satisfies the customer. People eat with their eyes; garnishes are meant to enhance the food, not to cover it up.

Key Terms

blanch   garnish

channel knife   zester

corer

As with any art, the key is to begin with the right tool for the job. A garnishing kit is an important component of a chef's collection of tools; it enables a chef to create attractive and functional **garnishes** (Figure 6-1). In some cases, garnishing tools are also used to reshape fruits and vegetables to create a uniform look.

FIGURE 6-1 Garnishes are used to enhance food.

Let's look at the components of a typical garnishing kit.

Tourne/ Peeling Knife

Tourne blades are curved and are usually 2″ to 3″ long (Figure 6-2). They are used to peel, slice, trim, and dice small fruits, vegetables, and cheese. This is the tool to use to produce the classical seven-sided potato (Figure 6-3).

FIGURE 6-2 A tourne knife.

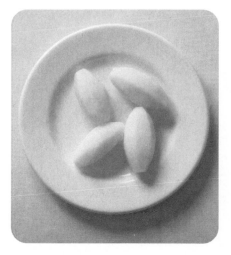

FIGURE 6-3   A tourne knife is used to create tournes.

Oval Melon Baller/ Parisienne Scoop

Melon ballers cut melons and other soft-fleshed fruits and vegetables into uniform oval shapes (Figure 6-4). They are also useful in creating cream cheese or butter balls. Most single melon ballers are available in 1 1/8" baller size.

FIGURE 6-4   Oval melon baller.

Double Melon Baller

A double melon baller has a baller at each end; one is 7/8", and the other end is larger, at 1". It can be used in the same manner as the oval melon baller but offers a choice of size (Figure 6-5, Figure 6-6, and Figure 6-7).

FIGURE 6-5   Double melon baller.

To create a melon ball, simply insert the baller into the melon's flesh. Twist the tool to form balls.

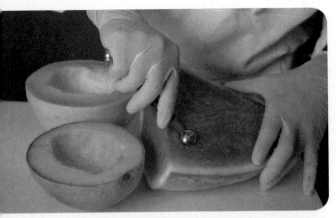

FIGURE 6-6 Using a melon baller.

FIGURE 6-7 A variety of melon balls.

Channel Knife

Use a **channel knife** to remove strips of peel or rind from fruits and vegetables (Figure 6-8). It can also be used for fluting mushrooms and making decorative cuts or channels in fruits and vegetables. The tool measures 6″ long. Use the channel knife to remove strips of skin, creating decorative grooves the length of the fruit or vegetable. Space the grooves evenly, leaving some peel or skin (Figure 6-9). Once the grooves have been made, slice the fruit or vegetable into disks (Figure 6-10).

FIGURE 6-8 Channel Knife

FIGURE 6-9 Making the grooves.

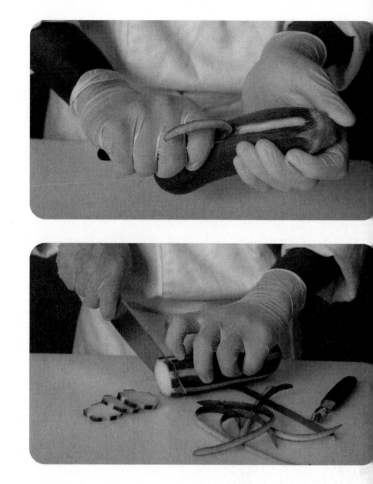

FIGURE 6-10 Slicing the cucumber chips.

Citrus Zester

The zest of oranges, lemons, and other citrus fruit is an important component of many recipes; it is also used as a garnishing ingredient. For example, a pinch of lime zest is the perfect garnish on top of a slice of key lime pie. Citrus **zesters** have five tiny cutting holes, which create threadlike strips of peel (Figure 6-11). This tool quickly creates fine zest from the rinds of any citrus fruit without including the bitter underlayer, called pith (Figure 6-12).

FIGURE 6-11 Citrus zester.

FIGURE 6-12 Zesters remove the zest, leaving behind the pith.

Zesters are sometimes used to remove thin strips from vegetables, such as zucchini or cucumbers. Try using the zester to create long, thin strands of carrot as a quick garnish for salads or soups. Firmly press as you draw the zester down along the skin of the fruit or vegetable.

Corer

Corers smoothly eject the core and seeds of an apple or a pear without disturbing the fruit's skin (Figure 6-13). To use, simply center the tool over the stem end of the fruit, push down firmly, and twist it, so that the serrated blade cuts through the meat (Figure 6-14). Retract the utensil and discard the core.

FIGURE 6-13 Apple corer.

FIGURE 6-14 Removing the apple's core and seeds.

Peeler

Peelers are included in most basic garnishing kits. Not only are they used to peel vegetables, such as potatoes or carrots, in preparation for cooking, but they can also be used to cut uniform strips of vegetables and fruits (Figure 6-15).

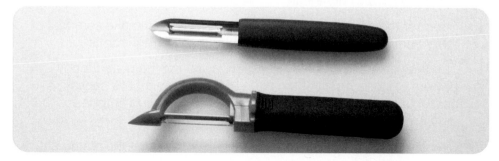

FIGURE 6-15   The peeler at the top of the frame is a European-style straight-edged peeler. The bottom peeler is a swivel peeler with a soft grip. Both peelers can perform the same functions. Which one you choose is a matter of personal preference.

Care of Garnishing Tools

Well-cared-for garnishing tools will last for many years. Always wash and sanitize them immediately after use. Let the tools air dry and then store them properly.

Never put your garnishing tools to soak in a sink, as their sharp edges can become a hazard for others who follow and use the soapy water. Also, the tools' sharp edges will dull if they are exposed to other utensils or are bumped against a stainless steel sink. It is not recommended that you put garnishing tools in the dishwasher. Because garnishing tools have sharp edges, it is best to store them in a carrying case.

Creating Garnishes

There are many reliable garnishing books that provide instructions for creating advanced-level garnishes for those wanting to learn beyond this basic introduction.

It's important to remember that the purpose of a garnish is to enhance a plate of food, both in appearance and in taste. Be careful not to overdo garnishes and to highlight the food appropriately by using the right garnish—in most cases, the simpler the better. We will present a few basic garnishes in this text.

Tips for Making Garnishes

- Use only firm, blemish-free fruits and vegetables.

- Consider the symmetry of the plate and use the appropriate size of fruit or vegetable.

- Always wash and dry the fruit or vegetable before creating the garnish.

- Consider the garnish's taste, color, and shape and make sure that all three elements enhance the food rather than detract from it.

- Size the garnish to fit the overall composition of the plated food. Beware of scale. Think of the plate of food as an artist's canvas. A garnish should add a punch of color to the plate and emphasize the food it is garnishing.

- Use garnishes that reflect the overall feel or theme of the restaurant, the dish, or the event.

Tomato Rings

1. Select a small, unblemished tomato, measuring 1 1/2" to 2" in diameter.

2. Wash and dry the tomato.

3. Cut off one end with a paring knife. Use a melon baller to remove the seeds and insides.

4. Cut off the opposite end, so that you have a tomato that resembles a napkin ring (Figure 6-16). Place it around a small bunch of chilled, tender green beans.

FIGURE 6-16 Tomato ring.

Citrus Rings

Citrus rings make a simple and elegant garnish. Use lemons, limes, or both. These can be used as napkin rings or they can encircle steamed vegetables, such as asparagus, broccoli spears, green beans, carrot sticks, and potato or sweet potato sticks.

1. Select firm fruit.

2. Wash and dry the fruit.

3. Cut it in half horizontally.

4. Remove the meat from the fruit; leave both halves of the peel intact.

5. Slice the remaining peel to create rings. The use will determine the needed width.

Tomato Roses

Most novices can master tomato roses in a few minutes. They are quick and easy to make (Figure 6-17). Tomato roses can be made ahead of time and refrigerated until service.

FIGURE 6-17   Tomato roses.

1. Select firm, medium-sized, blemish-free, ripe tomatoes.

2. Wash and dry.

3. Use a paring or tourne knife to peel off the skin, beginning at the top of each tomato, and peel around the circumference of the tomato. The peels should be in strips approximately 1″ wide, without much flesh

attached. Create a long, continuous peel. (Try to make it wavy as you cut around the tomato. That will help it look like a real rose.) Only one strip is used for each rose, so the longer the better.

4. To form a rose, roll one end of the peel tightly to make the center. Make sure that the peel side is down as you roll. The remaining peel can be loosely wrapped around the center. This will give the appearance of a real rose. Secure the bottom of the rose with a wooden toothpick.

5. Set the roll on a plate and arrange the "petals" of the rose. For an additional touch, place several mint leaves under the rose, so that they look like they are part of the rose.

Leek Ties

Leek ties can be used to tie a number of steamed vegetables together, adding a touch of class to a side dish or to any main entree (Figure 6-18). Try tying carrot sticks, asparagus, green beans, or potato or sweet potato sticks. Leek ties can also be tied around phyllo dough pouches or parchment packets filled with poached fish.

FIGURE 6-18   Leek ties.

1. Select a high-quality leek stalk.

2. Wash and dry.

3. With a paring knife, remove the long, green parts of the leek, which will be used as the tie. (Keep them as long as possible. It's best to tie the food first before cutting.)

4. **Blanch** the leek ends in boiling water (approximately five minutes).

5. Cool the leek immediately in ice cold water. Dry.

6. Using the leek end, tie a bow around the bundle of vegetables. Cut the ends to uniform lengths.

Green Onion Tassels

Green onion tassels make festive garnishes (Figure 6-19). Short onion "brushes" can also be made, using the same technique on a green onion that has been trimmed.

FIGURE 6-19   Green onion tassels.

1. Select good-quality green onion stalk.

2. Wash and remove the tough, dark green outer leaves.

3. Place the onion on a cutting board. Using a paring knife, make long cuts the length of the green portion of the onion. Repeat until it looks frilly.

4. Place in ice water and refrigerate. The frills will curl up in the ice water. Remove and dry before serving.

Chili Pepper Flower

Red jalapeno chilies can easily be transformed into flowers (Figure 6-20). While most restaurant patrons won't eat them, chili flowers are often used to garnish hot or spicy plated food. Be careful not to get any of the chili oil on your skin, as it will cause an uncomfortable burning sensation. (The American Culinary Federation recommends that gloves be worn whenever you are working directly with food that is not going to be cooked. Gloves should be worn when preparing most garnishes. It is imperative that gloves are worn when working with chili peppers.) Take special care not to rub your eyes when working with chilies.

FIGURE 6-20 Chili pepper flower.

1. Select unblemished chilies.

2. Wash and dry.

3. Beginning at the tip of the chili, make long slits, stopping within 1/2″ to 1″ of the stem with a paring knife. Evenly space the cuts around the chili.

4. Remove any seeds that are visible inside the chili.

5. Put the chili flower in a bowl of ice cold water and store in the refrigerator. It will open as it chills.

6. Remove the chili flower from the water and let it dry before using it as a garnish.

Radish Flower

Radishes make beautiful flowers in just a few minutes (Figure 6-21).

1. Select unblemished radishes. Trim off the root ends and wash thoroughly.

2. Use a paring knife to make thin slits around each radish. Stop before cutting through the stem end. Be sure to space the slits evenly around the radish.

3. Make another series of slits toward the center of the radish.

4. Place the radishes in ice water and store them in the refrigerator. The flower petals will open in the ice water. Remove and dry them before serving.

Knife Cuts

Dicing is cutting a product into cubes. A chef's knife is generally the preferred knife for this task. Dices range in sizes. The brunoise measures 1/8″ × 1/8″ × 1/8″; a small dice measures 1/4″ × 1/4″ × 1/4″ square; medium dice cuts measure 1/2″ × 1/2″ × 1/2″; and large dice cuts measure 3/4″ × 3/4″ × 3/4″.

A julienne cut is actually the beginning of a brunoise dice and is shaped like fine matchsticks measuring 1/8″ × 1/8″ × 1 to 2″.

A batonnet is the beginning of a small dice and is slightly larger than a julienne. It is 1/4″ × 1/4″ × 2 to 2 1/2″ long.

The classic French fry cut is a variation of the batonnet cut, which varies slightly in size. The blocks can measure anywhere from a 1/3″ to a 1/2″ and are usually 3″ long.

Chopping quickly produces odd-shaped cuts. It is the cut to use when size and shape are not important.

Use a chef's knife to chop herbs. Firmly hold the herbs with the opposite hand. Raise the knife handle up and down, using a rocking motion, with the tip of the knife acting as a hinge. Continue chopping until the herb is chopped as fine as you'd like.

To make a concassé : Remove the seeds, once the tomatoes have been peeled and halved.

Cut the tomato into fourths and chop.

Mincing is a fine chop cut made by using a chef's knife or mezzaluna. Use this cut on smaller products, such as garlic, fresh herbs, or ginger.

The paysanne is a decorative cut that is 1/2″ squares but is cut into 1/8″ slices, so it is thinner than a typical dice cut. The final dimensions are 1/2″ × 1/2″ × 1/8″. Paysanne is traditionally a square cut

A rondelle is a coin-shaped slice of a round vegetable, such as carrot or cucumber.

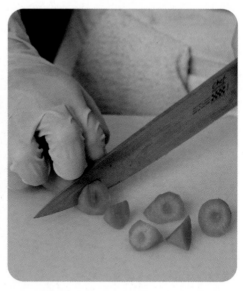

An oblique cut is used when you need additional flavors, and the appearance of larger cut vegetables as in stir-frying recipes.

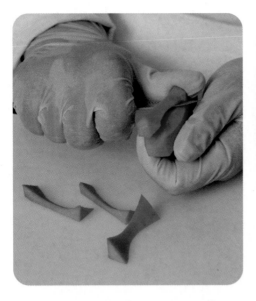

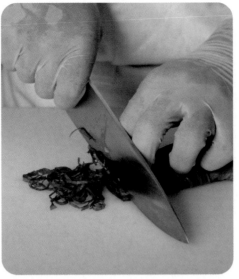

A tourne cut generally measures 2″ long, 3/4″ in diameter and will have seven sides. This cut produces barrel-shaped vegetables—perfect for any upscale side dish.

The chiffonade is a fine sliced or shredded cut which can be used for salads, sauces, and garnishes.

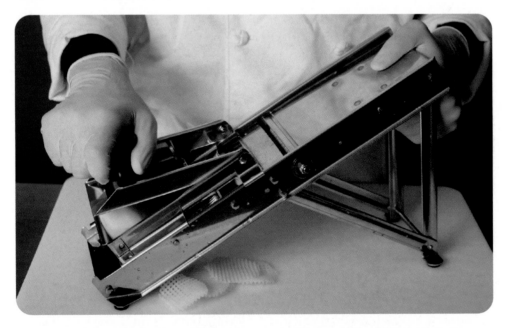

Use a mandolin to make the waffle cut known as the gaufrette. Make a first slice and then turn the product 90° and make a second cut. Turn the product to the original position and repeat with each cut.

Garnishes

Garnishes are used to decorate or embellish plated food items.

This prawn stuffed tomato appetizer plate is enhanced by the pea pod fan and onion tassel.

Onion flowers are easy to make. Simply cut several spring onion stalks into even slices. Use three slices that are about the same size. Place on plate with a caper in the middle.

Orange strips make a quick and effective garnish for this orange cream tart.

Slice gherkins nearly to the end and then fan for a nice garnish, perfect with any sandwich.

This seafood platter is garnished with a fluted lemon and parsley.

Lemon twists are aesthetic and functional.

Garnishing tools can be used to create unique fruit bowls. Here a fluted melon bowl is used to serve cold soup.

This is an overhead view of a watermelon made into a basket with a handle, containing balls of various melons.

Filo pastry parcels and dolmades are neatly tied with red pepper and green leek strips used as ribbons.

Rice and herb dolmades are tied with leek and pepper strips and garnished with cucumber twists and lemon curls.

Garnish roses can be made out of a number of vegetables including ginger, radishes, and tomatoes. This California sushi is garnished with pickled ginger rose and cucumber crest.

The tomato rose provides the focal point for the Oriental-style crab crepes that are garnished with prawns, lemon and lime wedges, and fresh dill and basil.

The outer bright red of the radish contrasts nicely with the white inside. Made into a radish rose, it adds a splash of color to this dish of tacos.

This succulent fried shrimp dish is prepared with a savory sauce and sesame seeds and placed beside a decorative white radish rose and parsley.

Garnishes should not be limited to appetizers and entrees. Think of creating garnishes for desserts and beverages as well. The strawberry fan adds a touch of class to this strawberry milkshake.

A melon basket with a scalloped edge containing mixed melon balls is an attractive dessert or salad is an easy way to dress up a fruit salad.

Vegetables including the tourneed carrots serve as a garnish for this goat cheese topped fillet steak served in a bed of pine nut sauce.

Chili pepper flowers complement the blue plate with cabbage salad, and barbecued Thai-style prawns.

This gourmet plate presentation showcases a steak with mushroom sauce that is topped with a fluted mushroom. The piped mashed potatoes are enhanced with a potato gaufrette.

Sometimes less is best. A touch of tomato concasse adds a punch of color to this plate of stuffed squid.

A bacon cheeseburger sits on a plate next to cherry tomatoes, carrot curls, and chips.

Chocolate curls are easily made with a vegetable peeler and a block of chocolate.

FIGURE 6-21 The photo shows two styles of radish roses. The flower on the left was described above. The second type on the right is made by starting in the center of the radish and making cuts to the outside edge. Space the cuts evenly.

Carrot and Cucumber Crest

Vegetable crests will augment any entree (Figure 6-22).

FIGURE 6-22 Vegetable crest.

1. Select high-quality cucumbers and carrots.

2. Wash and peel each carrot.

3. Use the peeler to peel off long, even sections of the cucumber peel.

4. Using a chef's knife, slice a carrot rondelle and then cut it into a crown shape with a paring knife. Note the straight bottom edge and the three sharp points at the other end, forming a "crown."

5. Do the same with the cucumber peel.

6. To form the crest, alternate five crowns, placing the cucumber and carrot in a semicircle.

7. Place one last carrot crown in the center of the five alternated crowns.

Carrot Knot

Carefully knotted carrot strips can add whimsical ornamentation to a variety of dishes (Figure 6-23).

1. Select firm carrots.

2. Wash and dry.

3. Peel.

FIGURE 6-23   Carrot knots.

4. Slice long (the longer the better, but at least 6″ long), 1/4″- to 1/2″-wide strips of carrot with a chef's knife.

5. Soak the strips in a solution of 2 cups water and 2 tablespoons salt until pliable.

6. Tie strips into square knots.

7. Chill in ice water.

8. Dry before serving.

Fluted Mushroom

Fluted mushrooms offer an interesting accompaniment to salads served cold. Or they can be sculpted and then brushed with butter and broiled for several minutes to accompany steak or a variety of hot dishes (Figure 6-24).

FIGURE 6-24   Fluted mushroom.

1. Select blemish-free mushrooms.

2. Thoroughly wash mushrooms under running water. If necessary, scrub any dirt off gently with a soft cleaning brush and let the mushrooms air dry.

3. Using a tourne knife held at a 45° angle, make thin, V-shaped grooves.

4. Work clockwise around each mushroom, making a groove about every 1/8".

5. Remove and discard the tiny triangles made from the groove. You can also choose to make fewer grooves; the key is to space them evenly around the mushroom cap.

6. If a star is to be added in the center of the mushroom, press the point of the knife in the center of the mushroom and make a five- or six-point star shape.

7. If serving the mushrooms raw, first dip them in lemon juice to prevent them from turning brown.

Carrot Curl

Carrot curls add color and texture to salads (Figure 6-25).

FIGURE 6-25 Carrot curl.

1. Select good-quality, long, straight carrots.

2. Wash and dry.

3. With a vegetable peeler, cut long, even strips of carrot—the longer and wider the better.

4. Roll the curls up and secure with a toothpick.

5. Place in water and refrigerate (Figure 6-26).

6. Before serving, drain the water off the curls and remove the toothpicks.

FIGURE 6-26 Place curl in water and refrigerate until served.

Fans

Cucumber Fans

Cucumber fans may look complicated, but they are quick and easy to make (Figure 6-27).

FIGURE 6-27 Channeled and sliced cucumber.

1. Select a firm, blemish-free cucumber.

2. Wash and dry.

3. Using a channel knife, score the cucumber vertically from end to end. Space the cuts evenly around the cucumber.

4. Cut off both ends with a chef's knife.

5. Begin slicing 1/8"- to 1/4"-thick slices, but don't cut all the way through the cucumber. Leave 1/4" of the flesh connected on the side to hold the rounds together.

6. Slice off the length of fan you want and place on a plate, spreading the fan open (Figure 6-28).

FIGURE 6–28 Spreading the fan open.

Fruit Fan

Fruit fans can be made with apples, pears (fresh or poached), or strawberries.

To help keep fresh pears and apples from turning brown, rub the cut surfaces with lemon juice or dip them into a small bowl of water mixed with the juice of one lemon.

Pears or Apples

1. Select firm, blemish-free fruit.

2. Wash and dry.

3. Peel the pear or apple, core it with an apple corer, and cut it in half with a chef's knife.

4. Make even cuts approximately 1/4" vertically. The key is to stop cutting about 1/2" before the bottom of the fruit. Keep the bottom intact.

5. Fan out the fruit (Figure 6-29).

FIGURE 6-29   Pear fan.

Strawberries

1. Select firm, blemish-free berries.

2. Wash and dry, leaving on the stems.

3. Using a paring knife, cut from the bottom of each strawberry to about 1/8″ from the top.

4. Make a series of similar cuts evenly spaced throughout the berry.

5. Fan out from the bottom of the berry (Figure 6-30).

FIGURE 6-30   Strawberry fan.

Citrus Fan

Add a touch of elegance to a lemon fan by first cutting strips around the lemon with a channel knife. Pull the channel knife through the peel from end to end, leaving about 1/4″ to 1/2″ between each cut.

1. Select blemish-free citrus fruit.

2. Score the sides with a channel knife.

3. Slice the lemon into disks approximately 1/8″ thick with a chef's knife.

4. Slice the disks in half.

5. Arrange half disks in a semicircle (Figure 6-31).

FIGURE 6-31 Citrus fan.

Citrus Twist

Any citrus fruit can make an appealing and colorful citrus twist (Figure 6-32).

FIGURE 6-32 Citrus twist.

1. Select firm, blemish-free fruit.

2. Wash and dry.

3. Use a preparing knife to cut the lemons into 1/8" to 1/4" slices. Take a wheel and make one cut (rind to center).

4. Twist the ends in opposite directions (Figure 6-33).

FIGURE 6-33 Preparing a citrus twist.

Citrus Butterfly

1. Select firm, blemish-free fruit.

2. Cut the fruit into thin, horizontal slices with a chef's knife.

3. For each slice, cut out a triangle at the top and one at the bottom. Discard the triangles. Before serving, twist the remaining part of the fruit slice (Figure 6-34). It will look like a butterfly.

4. Antennas can be made out of two strips of the peel and placed in the center of the butterfly.

FIGURE 6-34 Citrus butterfly.

Citrus Strip

Citrus strips offer an accent that adds color and an appealing citrus fragrance to any dish or dessert (Figure 6-35). Any citrus fruit can be used. Try lemon, lime, orange, tangerine, or grapefruit, or a combination of several types of fruit.

1. Select firm, blemish-free fruits.
2. Wash and dry.
3. Use a channel knife to make long, even strips.

FIGURE 6-35 Citrus strips.

Fluted Lemon

A fluted lemon or lime half makes an attractive, useful side for any fish or seafood entree (Figure 6-36).

1. Select firm lemon or limes that blemish-free.
2. Wash and dry.

FIGURE 6-36 Fluted lemon half.

3. Hold each fruit with the stem end up; hold the bottom end between your thumb and middle finger. With a paring knife, make a series of even sawtooth cuts all the way around the fruit. Make sure that the cuts are going to the center of the fruit.
4. Twist and pull the fruit apart to reveal two fluted or star garnishes.

Orange Curl

Add a twist of color and visual appeal with orange curls (Figure 6-37). They have a great aroma. (Any citrus fruit will do.)

1. Select firm, blemish-free fruit.

2. Wash and dry.

3. Use a channel knife or vegetable peeler to gently remove 1/4"- to 1/2"-wide strips. Make them as long as possible.

4. Wrap the strips tightly around chopsticks.

5. Let them stand at room temperature until they hold the curled shape.

6. Pull them off the chopsticks and cut into desired lengths.

FIGURE 6-37 Citrus curls.

Summary

Garnishes are meant to enhance plated food by adding color, composition, and overall design. Since people eat with their eyes, garnishes can increase appeal.

A basic garnishing kit contains a variety of tools. When properly cared for, the tools will last for many years.

Use firm, blemish-free fruits and vegetables for garnishes. Select the appropriate size to work with the symmetry of the plate and the food to be garnished. With a little practice and some talent, a chef can learn to make appetizing and visually appealing garnishes.

Chapter Review Questions

Short Answer

1. What is the main function of a garnish?

2. List the six basic tools that are generally found in a garnishing kit. (Treat the oval and double melon baller as one type of tool.)

3. Why is it important to use fruits and vegetables that are blemish-free for garnishes?

4. What cautions should be taken when working with chilies?

5. What can be done to prevent fluted mushrooms from turning brown?

Multiple Choice

6. A _____ tool is used to peel, slice, trim, and dice fruits and vegetables.

    a. channel knife

    b. tourne knife

    c. zester

    d. peeler

7. A _____ can remove the core and seeds of an apple without disturbing the fruit's skin.

    a. peeler

    b. channel knife

    c. corer

    d. baller

8. _____ can be used as napkin rings.

    a. Leek ties

    b. Carrot curls

    c. Orange curls

    d. Citrus rings

9. When making a leek tie, what should happen once the leek stalks are blanched?

    a. drain and dry

    b. place in the refrigerator to cool

    c. place in ice water

    d. discard tough, dark stalks

10. A _____ should be used to create carrot curls.

    a. peeler

    b. zester

    c. baller

    d. tourne knife

Culinarian's Code

I pledge my professional knowledge and skill to the advancement of our profession and to pass it on to those who are to follow.

I shall foster a spirit of courteous consideration and fraternal cooperation within our profession.

I shall place honor and the standing of our profession before personal advancement.

I shall not use unfair means to effect my professional advancement or to injure the chances of another colleague to secure and hold employment.

I shall be fair, courteous and considerate in my dealings with fellow colleagues.

I shall conduct any necessary comment on, or criticism of, the work of a fellow colleague with careful regard of the good name and dignity of the culinary profession, and will scrupulously refrain from criticism to gain personal advantage.

I shall never expect anyone to subject themselves to risks which I would not be willing to assume myself.

I shall help to protect all members against one another from within our profession.

I shall be just as enthusiastic about the success of others as I am about my own.

I shall be too big for worry, too noble for anger, too strong for fear and too happy to permit pressure of business to hurt anyone, within or without the profession.

Adopted by the American Culinary Federation, Inc., at its convention in Chicago, August 1957.

Appendix II

About the American Culinary Federation

Established in 1929, the American Culinary Federation (ACF) is the largest professional chefs' organization in North America. . .

ACF, which was the progeny of the combined visions of three chefs' associations in New York, N.Y., is comprised of more than 18,000 members in 240 chapters across the United States, and is known as the "authority on cooking in America." Its mission is "to make a positive difference for culinarians through education, apprenticeship and certification, while creating a fraternal bond of respect and integrity among culinarians everywhere." One of ACF's defining historical moments remains the ACF-led initiative that resulted in the upgrade of the definition of "chef" from domestic to professional in 1976.

ACF offers educational programs and opportunities for both the culinary student and professional culinarian. . .

ACF operates the only comprehensive certification program for chefs in the United States, awarding 14 different levels of certification. ACF is the only organization to offer master chef and master pastry chef certification, a program that launched in 1981. ACF also has a globally lauded apprenticeship-training program for cooks and pastry cooks, which began in 1976. Apprenticeship programs are usually for two or three years; however, ACF introduced a six-month training program in 2003 to provide greater training to current employees to enhance their skills and value to the operation. In addition to certification and apprenticeship, ACF provides accreditation to secondary and postsecondary culinary schools.

ACF holds numerous events that offer professional-development opportunities to ACF members of all levels. . . .

ACF annually hosts four regional conferences, a Central, Northeastern, Southeastern, and Western, which are held in various locations throughout the United States in an effort to reach chefs nationwide. The programs apply to all culinarians, from students to retiring chefs. ACF also holds a national convention to foster continued education and communication among culinarians at all levels. Its annual convention, first held in 1950 at the Lexington Hotel in New York, N.Y., is the largest gathering of professional culinarians in the nation.

ACF also works in tandem with two 501(c)(3) organizations, the American Culinary Federation Foundation (ACFF) and The Chef & Child Foundation (ACFCFF). . .

Two important groups under the ACFF include ACF Culinary Team USA, the culinary team that is the official representative of the United States in national and international competitions, and the American Academy of Chefs, the honor society of the ACF. ACF Culinary Team USA first competed in the world's premier international competition, the Internationale Kochkunst Ausstellung (IKA), or "culinary olympics," in Germany in 1956, and most recently was world champion in hot-food cooking at the 2004 IKA, and came in second in cold-food in the Salon Culinaire Mondial competition in Basel, Switzerland, in 2005. The team has established a reputation as the experts on American cooking worldwide.

The American Academy of Chefs, established in 1955, consists of nearly 800 accomplished chefs from ACF and around the globe whose mission is the education of future culinarians. To that end, AAC administers numerous scholarships through the American Culinary Federation Foundation to culinary students as well as professional chefs for continuing-education purposes. The AAC also has a Hall of Fame, established in 1988, which recognizes those chefs and AAC members who have excelled in the culinary profession and have dedicated a lifetime of service to the ACF and AAC.

Founded in 1989, The Chef & Child Foundation addresses the nutritional and dietary needs of children. Its mission is "to educate and assist the family in understanding proper nutrition and to be the voice of the American Culinary Federation in its fight against childhood hunger." ACFCCF programs include "Cooking Is for Kids," which teaches children about cooking, nutrition, and the foods of many cultures, as well as National Childhood Hunger Day national-awareness campaigns.

ACF's publishing outreach includes both print media and electronic mail. . .

ACF published its first official magazine, now known as *The National Culinary Review (NCR)*, in 1932. A monthly publication, NCR provides information on the latest food, menu, plating, and back-of-house management trends, as well as other issues of importance to chefs. ACF's official monthly newsletter, *Center of the Plate*, was launched in 1996, and highlights federation programs and accolades of ACF chapters and members. An additional print publication, *Sizzle: The American Culinary Federation Quarterly for Students of*

Cooking, was first published in 2004 and is the only magazine distributed nationally to 39,000 culinary and baking/pastry students. ACF's electronic newsletter, *ACF Today*, features the latest news and items of interest to ACF members, and is distributed to approximately 10,000 members bi-weekly.

ACF is the presidium of the eight-million-strong World Association of Cooks Societies (WACS) through 2007. . .

WACS is a global network of currently 72 chefs associations from around the world. Its mission is to maintain and improve the culinary standards of global cuisines through education, training, and professional development of its international membership. WACS is led by a president, vice president, treasurer, secretary general, and ambassador honorary president, as well as a board of continental directors. The WACS current president and vice president are ACF members as well as past ACF presidents.

Knife and Related Product Usage Chart

Knife	Use	Knife	Use
Chef's knife	Chopping; mincing; dicing and slicing	Meat fork	Lifting meats; anchoring meat when slicing or carving
Paring knife	Peeling; trimming; removing stems; garnishing	Kitchen scissors	Snipping; cutting; chopping
Boning knife	Deboning; fabrication; trimming fat or silverskin	Kitchen shears	Trimming; cutting through bones, fins, and feathers
Fillet knife	Removing skin and bones; cutting fillets and steaks	Honing steel	Honing knives
Slicer	Slicing; carving	Electric sharpener	Sharpening knives

Knife	Use	Knife	Use
Scimitar	Fabrication; cutting and portioning	Manual sharpener	Sharpening knives
Tourne knife	Trimming; peeling; and garnishing	Sharpening stone	Sharpening knives
Santoku	Chopping; mincing; dicing and slicing	Oval melon baller	Cutting into oval balls
Cleaver	Chopping and cutting through bones; trimming and dicing; use on its side for smashing	Double melon baller	Cuting into balls
Chinese cleaver	Chopping; mincing; dicing and slicing	Channel knife	Removing strips of skin
Clam knife	Opening clams and removing meat	Citrus zester	Removing zest
Oyster knife	Opening oysters and removing meat	Corer	Coring
Mezzaluna	Chopping	Peeler	Peeling
Mandolin	Cutting; slicing; julienning		

Basic Knife Cuts Chart

The graphics in this chart are the actual size. This guide can be used to measure your cuts.

Large Dice 3/4″ × 3/4″ × 3/4″

Medium Dice 1/2″ × 1/2″ × 1/2″

Small Dice 1/4″ × 1/4″ × 1/4″

Fine Brunoise 1/16″ × 1/16″ × 1/16″

Brunoise 1/8″ × 1/8″ × 1/8″

Batonette 1/4″ × 1/4″ × 2″ to 2 1/2″ long

Julienne 1/8″ × 1/8″ × 1″ to 2″ long

Paysanne 1/2″ × 1/2″ × 1/8″

Rondelle

Oblique

Tourne 2″ long and 3/4″ diameter

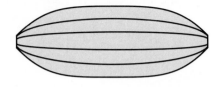

Anatomy of a Chef's Knife

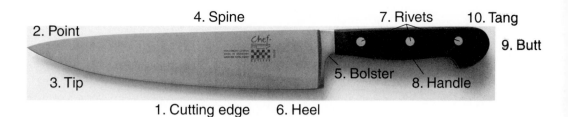

2. Point

4. Spine

7. Rivets

10. Tang

9. Butt

3. Tip

5. Bolster

8. Handle

1. Cutting edge

6. Heel

Appendix VI

Treating a Knife Wound

1. If possible, rinse the area with mild soap and tap water. Use an antiseptic wipe if running water isn't close at hand. If the wound appears to be deep, don't use soap or antiseptics that could damage underlying tissue.

2. Apply firm pressure directly over the cut with a sterile bandage or clean cloth. If blood soaks through the cloth, place another clean bandage over the top. Don't remove the blood-soaked layer until the bleeding completely stops.

3. Once the bleeding has stopped or slowed down significantly, apply an antibacterial ointment to coat the wound and prevent infection.

4. Cover with a bandage.

5. If the cut is on a finger, use a finger cot to keep the bandage from falling off and to offer additional protection to the wound.

When to Seek Professional Medical Help

Seek medical assistance if the wound is still bleeding after five minutes of firm pressure. You should also seek help if the wound appears to be deep, gaping, or badly torn. A doctor should also be consulted if the wound is dirty or embedded with foreign material (such as dirt or glass), shows any signs of infection, or causes a loss of movement or feeling in the affected area.

Appendix VII

Key to Review Questions

Chapter One

Short Answer

1. High-carbon stainless steel combines the benefits of both high-carbon steel and stainless steel. It provides a tough blade that has the ability to keep a very sharp edge. It is stain resistant and won't rust or discolor.

2. Henry Harrington's Dexter brand merged with John Russell's company to create Dexter-Russell, Inc., in 1933, which remains the largest knife manufacturer in the United States.

3. The forging process creates a stronger blade, with fewer impurities. Forged knives are heavier and provide a better balance in the hand. They are easier to sharpen and will last for years.

4. Gaps between the tang and the handle can provide a breeding ground for bacterial growth as food becomes trapped in the spaces. Uneven rivets can also irritate the chef's hand, causing blisters or sores and can snag or catch material.

Multiple Choice

5. b. iron

6. a. tenth

7. a. cutlers

8. b. nineteenth

9. c. Germany

10. b. was hard to sharpen

11. a. high-carbon stainless steel

12. b. point where the blade meets the handle

13. c. annealing

14. b. hardening

Chapter Two

Short Answer

1. Rivets should be flush with the handle to prevent injury to the hand or snagging on cloth. When rivets are tight, they prevent the establishment of a breeding ground for microorganisms, which can occur when there is space between the rivets and handle.

2. Most forged blades are made from one solid piece of high-carbon stainless steel. The steel is superheated and hammered with a forge into the basic shape of the blade. Most forged blades have a three-rivet handle and a full tang running the length of the handle. Forged blades generally have a bolster as well. Stamped blades are die-cut from conical steel, honed, and then polished. Stamped blades don't have a bolster and never have a full tang. They tend to be lighter and much less expensive than forged knives, which make them a popular choice as starter knives for some culinary students.

3. Slicers are available with straight, serrated, or granton blades. Straight slicers are considered the all-purpose option of the three. Straight slicers are best for cutting tenderloin, whole turkey, and chicken. Serrated slicers, also known as bread knives, are best for slicing breads and cakes or tomatoes. The serrated teeth prevent baked goods from being compressed when being cut. Granton slicers have slight indentations on the blade, making them the best choice for slicing whole roasts.

4. The carving knife has a long, slender blade that is very flexible. It is perfect for carving turkey, roast, and other large slabs of meat.

5. Meat forks are used to lift cuts of meat when roasting, grilling, sautéing, and anchoring the meat in place with one hand while slicing it with the other hand.

Multiple Choice

6. c. tang

7. a. tapered edge

8. d. chef's knife

9. b. boning knife

10. b. tourne

Chapter Three

Short Answer

1. Don't cut anything that is harder than the blade of the knife. Cut only on proper cutting surfaces. Don't put knives in drawers. Don't put knives in the dishwasher, where they can get nicked or affected by caustic cleaning materials.

2. Honing is the regular maintenance of the blade. It should be done every time the knife is used. Sharpening should take place when the knife won't keep a hone. Sharpening is the process of grinding the misaligned molecules of the blade. It is done with the use of a sharpening stone; as the blade is moved along the stone, the sharp edge returns.

3. Honing steels made of steel are magnetized, which helps the molecules resume their alignment. In addition, any metal particles that have been loosened during the honing process will cling to the steel and prevent the particles from getting into food.

4. A knife needs sharpening when the edge is lost with only the brief use of the knife and will no longer hold the hone.

5. Knives can be oversharpened. Oversharpening the blade will reduce the life of the knife and prematurely wear down the side of the blade and the bolster.

6. Water or oil will reduce the friction and heat created when the knife's blade strikes the stone.

7. Place the blade perpendicular to (at a 90° angle against) the shaft of the steel. Cut that angle in half, so that the blade is at a 45° angle, and then cut that in half again. That will leave the blade at a 22.5° angle, which is where it should be.

Multiple Choice

8. d. every time it is used

9. c. tang

10. c. the blade appears to be in good condition

11. d. until it is sharp

12. c. food-grade mineral oil

Chapter Four

Short Answer

1. Never use the same knife when switching from cutting meat to cutting vegetables or from raw to cooked foods unless the knife has been thoroughly washed, rinsed, and sanitized.

2. Place a damp towel or rubber cutting board liner underneath the cutting board to keep it from sliding around the countertop.

3. When handing another person a knife, place the knife down on the table or hand it to the person with the handle first.

4. Never soak a knife in the sink, because unsuspecting dishwashers or coworkers may reach down into the soapy water and get cut on the knife.

5. If blood soaks through the first cloth, place another bandage directly over the top of the first one. Do not remove the blood-soaked layer.

6. A doctor should be consulted when the wound is still bleeding after five minutes of firm pressure or if the wound appears to be deep, gaping, or badly torn. A doctor should also be consulted if the wound is dirty or embedded with foreign material, shows signs of infection, or causes a loss of movement or feeling in the affected area.

Multiple Choice

7. c. see how the knife feels when using it to cut food

8. a. away from your body

9. a. close to your body, pointed down

10. d. wash, rinse, sanitize, air dry, put away

Chapter Five

Short Answer

1. Large dice
2. Bias-cut rondelle
3. Gaufrette
4. Chiffonade
5. Tourne
6. Rondelle
7. Mince
8. Oblique
9. Julienne
10. French fry

Multiple Choice

11. c. 1/8″ × 1/8″ × 1/8″
12. d. paysanne
14. d. chef's
15. b. waffle

Chapter Six

Short Answer

1. Garnishes are edible accents that add visual appeal, drive sales, and satisfy customers. Since people eat with their eyes, garnishes are meant to enhance food.

2. The six basic tools are: tourne knife, baller, channel knife, zester, corer, and peeler.

3. Since the purpose of a garnish is to add visual appeal, only the freshest, most attractive pieces of fruit or vegetables should be used as a garnish.

4. Don't get any of the chili oil on your skin; it will cause a very uncomfortable burning sensation. Take special care not to get any of the oil in your eyes.

5. Dip fluted mushrooms in lemon juice to prevent them from turning brown.

Multiple Choice

6. b. tourne knife

7. c. corer

8. d. Citrus rings

9. c. place in ice water

10. a. peeler

Bibliography and Recommended Reading

American Culinary Federation. *Culinary Fundamentals.* Upper Saddle River, N.J.: Prentice Hall, 2006.

Bickel, Walter. *Hering's Dictionary of Classical and Modern Cookery,* 13th English ed. London: Virture, 1994.

Chon, Kye Sung, and Raymond T. Sparrowe. *Welcome to Hospitality.* Albany, N.Y.: Thompson Learning, 2000.

De Riaz. *The History of Knives.* New York: Crown Publishers, Inc., 1981.

Dornenburg, Andrew, and Karen Page. *The New American Chef*. Hoboken, N.J.: John Wiley & Sons, 2003.

Fortin, Jacques. *The Visual Food Encyclopedia*. Montreal: John Wiley & Sons, 1996.

International Life Sciences Institute. *A Simple Guide to Understanding and Applying the Hazard Analysis Critical Control Point Concept*. Washington, D.C.: ILSI Press, 1993.

Kittler, Pamela Goyan, and Kathryn P. Sucher. *Cultural Foods*, 3rd ed. Belmont, CA.: Thompson, 2001.

Labensky, Sarah R., and Alan M. Hause. *On Cooking*, 4th ed. Upper Saddle River, N.J.: Prentice Hall, 2007.

Labensky, Sarah R., Eddy Van Damme, Priscilla Martel, and Klaus Tenbergen. *On Baking*. Upper Saddle River, N.J.: Prentice Hall, 2005.

Labensky, Steven, Gaye G. Ingram, and Sarah R. Labensky. *Webster's New World Dictionary of Culinary Arts,* 2nd ed. Upper Saddle River, N.J.: Prentice Hall, 2001.

Loken, Joan K. *The HACCP Food Safety Manual*. New York: John Wiley & Sons, 1995.

Marriott, Norman G. *Principles of Food Sanitation,* 4th ed. Gaithersburg, Md.: Aspen,1999.

McGee, Harold. *On Food and Cooking*. New York: Scribner, 1984.

McSwane, David, Nancy Rue, and Richard Linton. *Essentials of Food Safety and Sanitation*, updated 4th ed. Upper Saddle River, N.J.: Prentice Hall, 2005.

National Assessment Institute. *Handbook for Safe Food Service Management*, 2nd ed. Upper Saddle River, N.J.: Prentice Hall, 1998.

National Restaurant Association Educational Foundation. *SerSave Coursebook*. New York: John Wiley & Sons, 2001.

Riley, Elizabeth. *The Chef's Companion*. Hoboken, N.J.: John Wiley & Sons, 2003.

Weaver, Merrill. *Foods: A Scientific Approach*, 3rd ed. Upper Saddle River, N.J.: Prentice Hall, 1998.

Glossary

Annealing—the heating and cooling process used in the manufacture of knives to prevent the blade from being brittle

Batonnet—the beginning of a small dice that measures 1/4 " x 1/4" x 2" long

Bias cut—a crosswise cut at a 45° angle; most often used in cutting vegetables for Oriental dishes

Blade—the part of the knife used for cutting

Blanch—to quickly cook a food in boiling water

Bolster—the point where the blade meets the handle

Boning—the process used to debone meat, poultry, and fish

Boning knife—a knife used for deboning poultry, trimming fat, and removing bones from meat and fish

Brunoise—a dice cut that measures 1/8" x 1/8" x 1/8"

Butterfly—to split meat in half with a knife without completely separating it, then spreading it open to look like a butterfly; commonly used for shrimp and chicken breasts

Carve—to cut or slice cooked meat, poultry, or fish into serving-size pieces using a carver, or carving knife

Carver, or carving knife—a knife used for slicing meat and poultry off the bones

Channel knife—garnishing tool used to remove strips of peel or rind from fruits or vegetables

Chef's knife—an all-purpose knife also known as a French knife

Chiffonade—a cut used to create fine slices of leafy vegetables or herbs

Chop—to cut food into small, uneven pieces

Clam knife—a knife with a blunt end; designed to open a clam shell

Cleaver—a knife used primarily for chopping or cutting through bones

Concassé (concasser)—small diced tomato squares that have been peeled and cored and the seeds have been removed

Corer—a sharp metal cylinder that removes the core and seeds of fruits, such as apples, without disturbing the outside of the fruit

Coring—removing the core or center of a fruit or vegetable using a corer or paring knife

Cross-contamination—the transfer of harmful organisms between items

Cube—to cut foods into cubes

Cutting board—a board made of plastic or wood used as a surface for cutting, slicing, and dicing food

Cutting edge—the bottom of a blade

Degrading—the manufacturing step in knife production that gives the knife its shape

Dice—a cube or square cut ranging from 1/16″ square cubes up to 3/4″ square cubes

Ergonomics—the applied science that studies safe and efficient movement

Fillet—to debone a piece of meat or fish

Fillet knife—a knife used to remove the flesh from whole fish or to cut steaks

Forge—the process used to treat metal in different steps to increase its hardness, density, and flexibility

French knife—another name for a chef's knife

Garnish—a secondary food used to enhance the primary food

Gaufrette—a lattice or waffle cut

Granton—a knife with semicircles that have been ground alternating into the sides of the blade, which keeps food from sticking to the knife

Grinding—creating an edge on a blade using a wheel that has a rough surface

HACCP (Hazard Analysis Critical Control Point)—a food safety program that focuses on potential problems in food preparation and service

Handle—the part of a knife usually made of wood, plastic, a combination of wood and plastic, or metal

Heel—the part of a knife below the bolster

High-carbon stainless steel—an alloy made of carbon and stainless steel; used to produce knives that won't rust or corrode; is easily sharpened and will hold its edge

Honing—realigning the microscopic teeth found on a knife's blade; generally done with a steel

Julienne—also called the matchstick cut, a cut that produces slender sticks of vegetables

Lamé—a knife used by bakers to score the top of a loaf of bread before it is baked

Mandolin (mandoline)—a hand tool with two adjustable blades; slices fruits and vegetables

Melon baller—a tool used to scoop round balls of the meat of melons

Mezzaluna—a curved blade with a handle; rocks back and forth and chops herbs, onion, and other vegetables

Mince—a fine, uneven cut or chop

Mineral oil—a food-grade mineral oil used as a lubricant on wet stones

Oblique—a food cut that produces pieces of food with two angle-cut sides

Oyster knife—a knife with a blunt end; is designed to open oyster shells

Pare—to remove the skin or rind of a fruit or vegetable using a paring knife

Paring knife—a knife used for small tasks, such as paring, mincing, and slicing small items

Parisian scoop—another name for a melon baller

Paysanne—a food cut that produces flat squares rather than cubes

Peel—to remove the skin or rind off a fruit or vegetable; similar to paring

Pocket roll carrier—a bag used to transport knifes; each knife has its own pocket and the case rolls up to form a round pouch

POM (polyoxmethelene)—a material used in the construction of durable knife handles

Rivets—metal pins used to hold the handle of a knife to the tang

Rondelle—a disk-shaped slice of round fruit or vegetable

Sanitizer—a chemical solution used to sterilize utensils and food preparation surfaces

Santoku—an Asian-inspired knife that is an alternative to the traditional chef's knife

Scimitar—a tool whose blade measures 12″ to 16″ long and is made for cutting raw meats and portioning them into a variety of cuts

Score—shallow even cuts in the surface of food used for decorative purposes in garnishing

Serrated—a knife blade edge that is wavy or jagged, similar to a saw's edge; used to cut things that are hard on the outside and soft on the inside, such as French bread

Shaft—a long spear used as the honing surface in a steel

Shank—another name for a bolster

Sharpening—making a knife's blade edge sharp

Sheath—an object designed to protect or cover a knife's blade

Shoulder carrier—a popular knife transporting system

Shredding—cutting food into flat, thin pieces of the same size

Slice—a piece of food that has been cut with a knife; to cut a piece of food

Slicer—a tool used for cutting tenderloin, whole turkey, or chicken; serrated slicers slice bread, cakes, and tomatoes; granton slicers are best for slicing whole roasts

Spine—the top of a blade, not the sharp side

Stamping—the process used to create knife blades by cutting them out of a flat sheet of metal

Steel—a rod made of steel or ceramic used in honing a knife blade between sharpenings

Tang—the metal that continues from a knife blade through the handle

Temper—to adjust the temperature of ingredients to a certain degree by heating or cooling and mixing or stirring

Tip—the very end of a knife blade

Tourne (tournée)—a cut that leaves a vegetable in the shape of a football with seven sides and blunt ends

Tourne knife—a knife with a curved blade used to make the classical cuts of seven-sided oblong pieces of vegetables

Trimming—removing fat from meat

Zester—a garnishing tool used to remove the zest of citrus fruit

Photo Credits

The majority of the photos in this book were taken by Jeff Hinckley. The knife manufacturing photos were taken in Germany by Mr. Schumacher and the photos for the accompanying posters were taken by Jim Smith. Additional photographers are listed below.

Cover: © Bettmann/CORBIS All Rights Reserved;
Fig 1-1: Neg./Transparency no. 39774. Courtesy Dept. of Library Services, American Museum of Natural History.;
Fig. 1-2: Dave King © Dorling Kindersley, Courtesy of The Museum of London;
Fig 1-3: Erich Lessing/Art Resource, N.Y.;
Fig 1-4: The Louvre, Paris. RMN: Reunion Musees Nationaux.;
Fig 1-5: Peter Hayman © The British Museum;
Fig. 1-6: © Judith Miller / Dorling Kindersley / Wallis and Wallis;
Fig 1-7: Getty Images Inc. - Hulton Archive Photos;
Fig 1-21: Melanie Acevedo/Corbis/Bettmann;
Fig 2-8: Dave King © Dorling Kindersley;
Fig 3-CO: Richard Embery/Pearson Education/PH College;
Fig 3-9: Richard Embery/Pearson Education/PH College;
Fig 5-2: David Murray and Jules Selmes © Dorling Kindersley;
Fig 5-5: David Murray and Jules Selmes © Dorling Kindersley;
Fig 5-9: Richard Embery/Pearson Education/PH College;
Fig 5-15: Corbis Digital Stock;
Fig 5-17: David Murray and Jules Selmes © Dorling Kindersley;
Fig. 5-18: David Murray and Jules Selmes © Dorling Kindersley;
Fig 5-20: Richard Embery/Pearson Education/PH College;
Fig 5-26: Richard Embery/Pearson Education/PH College;
Fig 5-27: Richard Embery/Pearson Education/PH College;
Fig 5-28: Richard Embery/Pearson Education/PH College;
Fig. 5-53: Richard Embery/Pearson Education/PH College;
Fig 5-54: Richard Embery/Pearson Education/PH College;
Fig 5-55: Jerry Young © Dorling Kindersley;
Fig 5-56: Jerry Young © Dorling Kindersley;
Fig. 5-57: Jerry Young © Dorling Kindersley;
Fig 6-1: © Dorling Kindersley;
Fig 6-17: David Murray and Jules Selmes © Dorling Kindersley;
Fig 6-18: © Dorling Kindersley;
Fig 6-19: © Dorling Kindersley;
Fig 6-20: © Dorling Kindersley;
Fig 6-22: David Murray and Jules Selmes © Dorling Kindersley;
Fig 6-23: © Dorling Kindersley;
Fig 6-24: Jerry Young © Dorling Kindersley;
Fig 6-25: © Dorling Kindersley;
Fig 6-26: David Murray and Jules Selmes © Dorling Kindersley;

Fig. 6-27: Jerry Young © Dorling Kindersley

Fig 6-28: David Murray and Jules Selmes © Dorling Kindersley;

Fig 6-29: Jerry Young © Dorling Kindersley;

Fig 6-30: © Dorling Kindersley;

Fig 6-31: © Dorling Kindersley;

Fig 6-32: © Dorling Kindersley;

Fig 6-33: © Dorling Kindersley;

Fig 6-34: © Dorling Kindersley;

Fig 6-35: David Murray © Dorling Kindersley;

Fig. 6-36: © Dorling Kindersley;

Fig. 6-37: David Murray and Jules Selmes © Dorling Kindersley;

Color Insert:

CI-07a: David Murray and Jules Selmes © Dorling Kindersley;

CI-07b: David Murray and Jules Selmes © Dorling Kindersley;

CI-07c: David Murray and Jules Selmes © Dorling Kindersley;

CI-07d: David Murray and Jules Selmes © Dorling Kindersley;

CI-08a: Luis Ascui © Dorling Kindersley;

CI-08b: © Dorling Kindersley;

CI-09a: Diana Miller © Dorling Kindersley;

CI-09b: Jerry Young © Dorling Kindersley;

CI-10a: David Murray and Jules Selmes © Dorling Kindersley;

CI-10b: David Murray and Jules Selmes © Dorling Kindersley;

CI-11a: David Murray and Jules Selmes © Dorling Kindersley;

CI-11b: David Murray and Jules Selmes © Dorling Kindersley;

CI-12a: Colin Fisher/Pearson Education Corporate Digital Archive;

CI-12b: Allen Polansky/The Stock Connection;

CI-13a: Jonelle Weaver/Getty Images, Inc. – Taxi;

CI-13b: David Murray © Dorling Kindersley;

CI-14a: David Murray and Jules Selmes © Dorling Kindersley;

CI-14b: Dave King © Dorling Kindersley;

CI-15a: John A. Rizzo/Getty Images, Inc.- Photodisc;

CI-15b: Martin Brigdale © Dorling Kindersley;

CI-16a: Picture Perfect USA, Inc.;

CI-16b: David Murray © Dorling Kindersley

Index

Index